Berlitz

Salzburg

D1337479

Front cover: Old Town rooftops

Right: The *Echte Salzburger Mozartkugel*, a chocolate delicacy

Festung Hohensalzburg • The fairy-tale castle dominates the city it was built to defend *(page 28)*

Old Town • A Baroque treasure trove, with sights including the stunning cathedral *(page 34)*

Residenzplatz • The most impressive square in the Old Town *(page 39)*

Grossglockner High Alpine Road • This twisting and turning route is one of the world's great scenic drives *(page 73)*

Hellbrunn Palace and Gardens — See the grand scale of living of Salzburg's prince archbishops (page 60)

St Peter's Abbey — The city's spiritual heart and the oldest active monastery in Austria (page 34)

Mozart's Birthplace — The house in which he was born is now a museum (page 43)

Mirabell Palace and Gardens — Built for the mistress of an archbishop, here you'll find opulence on a grand scale (page 54)

Königssee — Take a boat trip across the still waters of this beautiful Bavarian lake not far from Salzburg (page 68)

Museum of Modern Art — This showcase for contemporary art also offers a great view of the city (page 48)

CONTENTS

Introduction 7

A Brief History 12

Where to Go 27

A ➤ in the text denotes a highly recommended sight

The Mönchsberg and Environs.............. 27

*The Festung Hohensalzburg 28, Nonnberg
Convent 31, Nonntal District 33*

The Old Town.................................... 34

*St Peter's Abbey 34, Kapitelplatz 36,
The Cathedral 37, Residenzplatz 39,
Mozartplatz 41, Alter Markt 42, Getreidegasse 43,
Festival District 44, Around Gstättengasse 46,
Museum of Modern Art 48, Mülln 49*

The New Town 50

*Linzergasse 50, St Sebastian's Church 50,
Makartplatz 51, Mirabell Palace and Gardens 54,
Kapuzinerberg 57*

Salzburg's Environs............................ 58

*Leopoldskron Lake and Palace 58, Hangar-7 59,
Stiegl's Brauwelt 60, Hellbrunn Palace 60,
Klessheim Palace 63*

South of Salzburg............................. 64

*Untersberg 64, Berchtesgaden 67, Königssee 68,
Hallein 70, Werfen 71, Eisriesenwelt 72,
The Grossglockner Road 73, Krimml Waterfalls 76*

The Salzkammergut............................ 77

Fuchlsee 77, Wolfgangsee 78, Mondsee 81

59

41

53

What to Do 83

Culture and Nightlife 83

Shopping 87

Sports 89

Salzburg for Children 92

Eating Out 94

Handy Travel Tips 104

Hotels and Restaurants 128

Index 143

Features

The Salzburg Card 9
The Prince Archbishops. 16
Mozart in Salzburg. 20
Historical Landmarks 25
Johann Michael Rottmayr. 38
A Controversial Statue 41
The Mozarteum 52
Salzburg and The Sound of Music 56
The Föhn. 63
Legends of the Untersberg 66
Winter Wonderland 85
Calendar of Events. 93
Austrian Fast Food 99

37

67

103

INTRODUCTION

First-time visitors to Salzburg are often awed by the consistent dignity and style of the city's Baroque architecture. And rarely is a city so delicately worked into a dramatic natural setting. Rising above Salzburg's skyline and visible for kilometres around is the Festung Hohensalzburg, a fortress that sits atop the Mönchsberg mountain and watches over the city.

Below, the Altstadt (Old Town) is dominated by Baroque towers and church spires, built by a succession of independent bishops from the 16th to the 18th centuries. This historic centre became a Unesco World Heritage Site in 1996, recognised as an important European ecclesiastical area.

Salzburg is most famous for being the birthplace of Wolfgang Amadeus Mozart and, of course, as the setting for *The Sound of Music*, but the city's wealth of culture extends beyond that. With Easter and Whitsun festivals, as well as Mozart Week in January and the internationally known Salzburg Festival in summer, this is one of the world's top festival cities, vying with Vienna as the cultural capital of Austria.

Fiakers (horse-drawn carriages) are a sedate way to get around

Salzburg also hosts renowned Christmas markets in December, when the city is transformed into a winter wonderland, with ice sculptures, ice rinks, music, stalls and copious amounts of *Glühwein* (mulled wine).

Shoppers on the Getreidegasse, one of the city's oldest streets

Salzburg and the Salzach River

Geography and Climate

Salzburg is in the west of central Austria and close to the Bavarian border of Germany, in the northern foothills of the Alps. The city lies between two craggy hills, the Mönchsberg and the Kapuzinerberg, and is divided in two by the Salzach River. This was the life-blood of Salzburg for many centuries, used for transporting salt *(Salz)*, gold and copper mined in the mountains, and bringing much wealth to the city during the Middle Ages. Only a few kilometres from the city centre lies the closest real mountain, the Untersberg (1,853m/6,078ft).

Salzburg is influenced by the alpine climate, and generally has cold, dry, snowy winters and warm summers with a considerable amount of rain. When it rains here, it really pours. The locals call it *Schnürlregen* – 'string rain'. Whatever the season, the weather can be turned on its head by the warm south wind known as the *Föhn (see page 63)*.

Politics and Religion

Home to approximately 150,000 people, Salzburg is the capital of the province of the same name (pop. 520,000). It is one of Austria's youngest provinces, not incorporated into the country until 1816 (it was previously an independent ecclesiastical state). Austria is a federal state made up of nine provinces, each with its own local government. The Regional Assembly of Salzburg, elected every five years by proportional representation, consists of 36 members who have considerable influence over the politics and economics of the region.

While the role of the church in Salzburg is by no means what it was in the era of prince archbishops, the diocese continues to be one of the most important in the Roman Catholic Church, and the archbishop has direct access to the Pope. The Catholic Church remains a powerful local institution – of the city's 43 churches, 40 of them are Catholic – and owns a lot of land in and around the city, with the final say on where street music, open-air festivals and sporting

The Salzburg Card

A useful money-saver for the serious sightseer is the Salzburg Card, which allows free use of public transport, including the fortress funicular and sightseeing boat, as well as discounts for various cultural events, tours and excursions. It also serves as an admission ticket to the city's most important cultural sights, including Mozart's birthplace, the Hohensalzburg fortress, the Residenz Gallery, the Museum of Modern Art and the Baroque Museum in the Mirabell Gardens. Sights outside the town include Hellbrunn Palace, the open-air museum in Grossgmain, the salt mines of the Dürrnberg, and the cable-car trip at Untersberg.

Cards are valid for 24, 48 or 72 hours and cost May–Oct 24, 32 or 37, Nov–Apr 21, 29 or 34 – half price for children up to 15. You can buy the Salzburg Card from hotels, tobacconists and municipal offices.

events can take place. It also has the right to a claim a yearly tax from every citizen's salary to help with its upkeep (this tax also extends to other denominations too). Nevertheless, although more than two-thirds of the population counts themselves as Catholic, not many are regular church-goers.

Being a Salzburger

Salzburgers have a reputation for being aloof, and intimacy is reserved for their own close social circles. They are conservative in nature, though the younger generation is breaking the mould, becoming more outgoing and embracing influences from other cultures, especially on the music and entertainment scene. But this

The most famous Salzburger

does not reflect the whole picture, and citizens are in general very friendly towards tourists. If you're staying in Salzburg for more than a few days, expect to be recognised and greeted by people as you walk the streets. Salzburgers in the main love their city and are delighted when foreign visitors express appreciation of its appearance.

Laws are for obeying in Salzburg: litter is prohibited, jaywalking is not tolerated (if you transgress, expect a lecture or a look of disdain at the very least), crime is almost non-existent and the police operate a zero-tolerance policy. This might sound heavy-handed, but walking home at night is usually safe, disturbances on the streets are very rare and pick-pocketing occurs only in crowded bars.

Salzburgers enjoy a leisurely pace of life. They do a lot of walking – not of the brisk kind – and they frequent coffee houses, beer gardens and taverns, relaxing and watching the world go by. There is no sense of urgency here and certainly not the hectic pace that can be felt in other cities of a

Traditional felt hats

similar size. Salzburgers are passionate about their dogs, taking their faithful friends everywhere – into restaurants, the hairdressers, on the bus.

Salzburg is a university town with a good nightlife scene. The city is dotted with wine bars and taverns where you can enjoy fine Austrian wine and beer (the city has one of the country's best breweries in Stiegl's Brauwelt). The main areas for socialising by night are along Rudolfskai, Gstättengasse and Kaigasse, although there are many taverns scattered throughout the city. The Augustiner Brewery is also a must when visiting the city, with its fine beer halls and huge, tree-lined, summer beer garden.

No matter what time of year you visit Salzburg, there is always something happening, from the street-café way of life in the summer to the harvest festivals of the autumn, from the Christmas markets and winter skiing to *Fasching* and Easter festivals in the spring. The beauty of the city is enhanced with each season, making Salzburg a perfect year-round destination.

A BRIEF HISTORY

Salzburg's strategic location, near to one of the passes running from north to south through the Alps, brought the city power and prosperity through trade – especially of locally mined salt. But it also brought the city into conflict, as the valley was a major trading route from Italy to Germany.

Neolithic and Celtic Developments

The history of human activity in the Salzburg region can be traced back 6,000 years to the New Stone Age and a settlement on the Rainberg (behind the Mönchsberg). During the Bronze Age, around 1000BC, the Illyrians settled here, lured by the copper that was mined on the Mitterberg, near Bischofshofen. But in the centuries that followed, salt mining

A reconstructed Celtic farmstead in Hallein

became the primary industry, with mines at Hallstatt and later on the Dürrnberg, near Hallein. By around 500BC, the Celts had invaded the region and begun to mine salt and to build fortified settlements scattered around the hills. The area became a trading centre and the river was used to transport the salt, a valuable commodity.

Roman Occupation

Around 15BC, the Romans marched into the area, conquered the Celtic kingdom of Noricum and built a road over the Alps to Vivium (today's Klagenfurt). Known as Juvavum, the town acquired the status of a Roman

Latin inscription

When the foundation for the statue of Mozart was about to be laid in 1841, a marble floor was uncovered bearing the Latin inscription: 'Here lies happiness. Let no evil enter.'

municipium in AD45 and became the seat of one of the largest administrations outside Rome. Its focal point, the Forum, was quite likely to have been situated where Residenzplatz is today. During the reconstruction following World War II, the remains of a huge Roman temple were discovered in the Kaigasse area where the Kasererbräu hotel now stands.

Around AD500, the Baiuvari (Bavarians) laid waste to the city, after the Roman army stationed here had been laid low by an epidemic. They drove out the residents and set Juvavum's wooden structures alight. The ensuing conflagration destroyed most of the settlement, and was the cue for the Romans to withdraw from the province of Noricum.

Church and State Combined

Around 696, Bishop Rupert of Worms arrived as a missionary in Bavaria, whose ruler Duke Theodor granted him an area of land, including the remains of Juvavum. Here, Rupert founded the Monastery of St Peter and the Nonnberg Convent. Both institutions remain today, St Peter's as the oldest continuously active monastery in the Roman Catholic Church and the convent as the oldest surviving religious community for women.

Salzburg became a bishopric in 739 and, in the years that followed, one of the most important areas outside the Vatican. Among the early bishops of note was Virgil, responsible for the town's first cathedral in the mid-8th century. In 798 Salzburg was elevated to the status of an archbishopric by Pope Leo, and Abbot-Bishop Arno was promoted to archbishop and a prince of the Holy Roman Empire.

In 996, Emperor Otto III awarded Salzburg a town charter and the right to levy customs duties and mint its own coins. Less than a century later, during the power struggle between the Holy Roman Emperor and the Pope, Archbishop Gebhard of Salzburg weighed in on the side of Pope Gregory II. As protection against the imperial armies, he commissioned the fortresses of Hohensalzburg, Hohenwerfen and Friesach.

Growth and Destruction

Under the reign of Konrad I during the 12th century, the Hohensalzburg fortress was developed into a heavily fortified bastion. The high walls that he added can still be seen today.

But the fortress was not able to prevent the events of 1167, when Frederick Barbarossa's troops set fire to the city during a dispute with the Pope (Salzburg sided with the Church), destroying the cathedral. In the years that followed, Salzburg was rebuilt under the direction of Archbishop Konrad III. He also started construction of an immense new cathedral.

By the 13th century, the salt that was mined in Hallein was proving to be increasingly important for the region. The mines produced so much that Salzburg could drop the price considerably, giving the city a trading advantage over the competition from the neighbouring salt mines in Bad Reichenhall and Berchtesgaden. This added to the strength of the

Salzburg archbishops who, once they had procured a monopoly on salt trading, were able to raise the prices again.

Although the archbishops had been imperial princes since the 12th century, the areas they ruled were still considered to be part of the Duchy of Bavaria. In the early 14th century, in the machinations between the Bavarian and Austrian royal houses, Archbishop Friedrich III of Salzburg sided with the Austrian Friedrich I ('the Handsome'). Civil war raged for seven years until Louis IV of Bavaria won the decisive battle of Mühldorf in 1322. Although Salzburg had been on the losing side, the result of this internecine strife was that Bavaria was forced to concede its independence. In 1328, Salzburg became an autonomous state, separate from both Bavaria and Austria. However, the city's prosperity was soon to suffer another blow when the plague hit it in 1348, killing around 30 percent of the population.

During the late 14th and early 15th centuries, the traders of Salzburg grew in importance. It was during this period that many of the merchants' houses that survive today in the 'old' and 'new' towns were built. Archbishop Leonhard von Keutschach ruled Salzburg from 1495 to 1519, adding significantly to the size and impregnability of the fortress.

The town hall dates from the 15th century

The Peasants' War

Keutschach's successor, Matthäus Lang von Wellenberg, exerted political influence far beyond the boundaries of Salzburg. He was a cardinal, a councillor of Emperor Maximilian I and a politician with wide influence. He was decisive in the election of the Medici Pope Clemens VII, and the Habsburg Karl V would never have become emperor without his intervention. But it was on home ground that he faced his sternest challenge.

Salzburg's peasants were restless, suffering from increased taxation and the demands made on them by the nobility and monasteries. Inspired by Martin Luther, they also came to resent the hard-line Catholicism and apparent arrogance of

The Prince Archbishops

For more than 1,000 years, Salzburg and its surrounding territories were ruled by prince archbishops: men highly placed in the Holy Roman Empire and wielding great influence. They could depend on the power of the Church to back their causes, commendable or not. And they controlled just about everything: tax collection, land ownership, mining rights, the building of churches, monasteries and places of learning, the armies and, of course, the salvation of souls.

The Church and the state were not separate entities, and the prince archbishop, as the title implies, was at the head of both – usually a head of state first and a religious leader second. The prince archbishop of Salzburg was elected to the position; he was not appointed by the Pope or the Holy Roman Emperor, nor was his position a hereditary title. Indeed, these leaders were not allowed to marry – but that did not stop many of them taking mistresses and having numerous children. Normally, the youngest son of a noble family was nominated for the post.

The prince archbishops displayed varying degrees of benevolence. Many were patrons of the arts, as well as being responsible for the design and development of the city, including the iconic fortress.

their archbishop. In May 1525, they rebelled; the miners of Gastein joined in. The revolt spread beyond the borders of Salzburg, into adjacent Carinthia and Styria, both ruled by the Habsburg dynasty. On 4 June the rebels seized control of Salzburg, and briefly controlled the city as well as parts of Carinthia, Carniola and Upper Austria. Archbishop Matthäus negotiated an agreement with the rebel leaders, which adressed some of their demands. He promised them a council that

Archbishop Wolf Dietrich von Raitenau

would address their grievances, and the peasants broke off their siege of the Hohensalzberg fortress.

But in December 1525, Archbishop Matthäus felt secure enough to act more forcefully. He had a number of rebel leaders arrested and executed. The promised council met in January 1526, but was dissolved without achieving anything. The peasants resumed their revolt, joining forces with the Tyrolean revolutionary Michael Gaismair. But Matthäus, too, had allies, notably the Swabian League, and a force of 10,000 soldiers. There were a number of indecisive battles in May and June 1526, until the rebels were finally defeated at Radstadt.

Matthäus overcame the threat posed by the peasants with a combination of patience, determination, deceit and outside help. Though the Salzburg peasantry continued to lean towards the Lutheran Reformation, Archbishop Matthäus and his successors remained steadfast Catholics, developing a style of absolute rule directed against Salzburg's Protestant elements.

The City Takes Shape

Wolf Dietrich von Raitenau was elected in 1587. He was a man of great vision who began to oversee the architectural design of Salzburg as we know it today, bringing Italian Baroque style to the city. He tore down the 'undesirable' areas and in their place built wide, open squares and magnificent residences. Schloss Mirabell was built for his mistress, Salome Alt, who is said to have borne him between 12 and 15 children. His reign came to an end when he quarrelled over mining rights with the prince of Bavaria, whose army attacked Salzburg. Dietrich lost his allies and the support of the Church because of his affair with Salome Alt. Attempting to flee the city, he was captured and imprisoned in the Hohensalzburg fortress, the very building that was designed to protect him.

His nephew and successor was Markus Sittikus. Even though his reign as archbishop lasted only seven years from 1612 to 1619, Sittikus is credited with continuing the reconstruction of Salzburg that Dietrich had begun, and also instigating new projects such as the palace and gardens in Hellbrunn. He also laid the foundation stone for the cathedral that dominates Salzburg today.

Sittikus' successor, Paris Graf von Lodron, is acknowledged as Salzburg's greatest prince archbishop. He was elected in 1619 at the start of the Thirty Years' War, the religious battle between Catholics and Protestants. He

Fountain fun

Markus Sittikus is noted for installing the famous water fountains in Hellbrunn Palace. He used to enjoy inviting guests to dinner at the palace and dining outside at the stone table that survives today. He had little water fountains installed in each seat (except his own, of course) and at a given signal, they were turned on, to the discomfort of his guests and the amusement of their host.

managed to keep Salzburg out of the dispute, maintaining neutrality and preserving the dominance of the Catholic Church. This was a major achievement as the war left most of Central Europe devastated. During Graf Lodron's 34-year reign, Salzburg's population rose from 40,000 to 80,000. A great believer in education, he founded the university in 1623. He brought new wealth to the city by imposing tolls on traders using the nearby Pass Lueg, and he also expanded the mining and mineral trade of the region. His body was laid to rest beneath the dome of the cathedral.

Music mural in Archbishop Sittikus' Hellbrunn Palace

The End of the Prince Archbishops

The prince archbishops' dominance over the land of Salzburg ended at the beginning of the 19th century. In 1800, Napoleon defeated the Austrians at the Battle of Marengo and crossed the Alps at the head of a 40,000-strong army, while another French army crossed the Rhine, captured Munich and pushed on to take Linz in Austria. In the years that followed, as the European powers challenged Bonaparte on several fronts, Salzburg was bounced around between its larger neighbours.

From 1803 to 1805, Salzburg was an electorate of the Holy Roman Empire of German nations. The religious principality was secularised, and the political authority of the prince

Mozart in Salzburg

In 1737, Wolfgang's father Leopold Mozart arrived in Salzburg and en-rolled at the university, though shortly afterwards due to his obsession with music he was expelled because he neglected his studies. In 1743, he was accepted into the court orchestra and in 1747 married a local woman, Anna Maria Pertl. The couple had seven children, though only two survived, Maria Anna, known as Nannerl, and Wolfgang Amadeus (christened Joannes Chrysostomus Wolfgangus Theophilus), born in 1756. Leopold began to tutor Nannerl and this eventually became a point of interest and entertainment for young Wolfgang. As Leopold re-alised his children's talents, he began to spend more time with them, teaching them music with strict discipline and guidance. Mozart excelled at the clavier and was already composing little pieces before the age of five. At six, Mozart accompanied his father on tour, astounding the au-diences with his skills. Then, aged only eight, he went to London and per-formed in front of King George III, dedicating six sonatas to the queen (for which he received 50 guineas). When Mozart played in Italy at the age of 14, the Italians were so amazed by him that they announced the ring on his finger to be a talisman. Obligingly, Mozart removed it and pro-ceeded to play even more beautifully than before.

The prince archbishop at this time was Sigismund von Schrattenbach, who had a genuine interest in music. He funded the Mozart family's trips and allowed them to use court titles. It is no wonder that, after all the excitement of international adulation, young Mozart found his home town 'dull and boring'. Sigismund died in 1771 and was succeeded by Archbishop Colloredo, who had little interest in the arts and considered musicians to be among the lowest ranking courtiers. He put an end to the support of the Mozart family, halting their tours, and instead required that they stay in Salzburg and perform to the court. Mozart grew rest-less and left Salzburg for good at the age of 25. He moved to Vienna after a major row with the archbishop and his secretary.

archbishops finally came to an end. As part of the 1805 peace treaty of Pressburg, Salzburg was incorporated into Austria. The independent state was now a province of a large empire – but not for long. The Habsburgs declared war on France in 1809, but were defeated. This brought Salzburg under direct French administration for a year and a half. But in

Mozart with father and sister

1810, the area as far as the Leuken valley (Kitzbühel) was ceded to Napoleon's ally Bavaria. Salzburg's university was suspended and in 1811 the regional assembly was dissolved.

Following Napoleon's disastrous Russian campaign, Bavaria shrewdly switched its allegiance, and the Salzburgers found themselves once again in opposition to France. By 1814, Napoleon was being attacked on all fronts, and by the end of the year, he had been deposed and banished to Elba. The Great Powers – Austria, Prussia, Russia and Britain – convened the Congress of Vienna, at which the map of Europe was redrawn. Among many other realignments of territories, the Tyrol and Salzburg were assigned to the Habsburg rulers, and in 1816 Salzburg formally became part of Austria.

For the next 100 years, the ruling family left Salzburg to its own destiny, with limited funding and sparse resources to develop the city. The Habsburgs had little interest in residing there and likewise little interest in investing in the city. This turned out to be the saviour of Salzburg's distinctive appearance. Instead of knocking down and reconstructing buildings and infrastructure, there was no other choice than to repair and maintain what today is a vital part of its culture and history.

Early 20th Century

At the beginning of World War I, 49,000 Salzburgers were conscripted into the Austrian army to fight alongside Germany; 6,000 of them were killed and many more taken prisoner. Salzburg itself saw no battles, but the population suffered great hardship because of the lack of supplies. In 1918, the so-called 'rucksack war' broke out. Thousands of people, mostly women, set off for the outlying provinces in search of food for their families. Many were caught by the local authorities and charged with black-marketeering. At the end of World War I, the Habsburg monarchy was abolished and Austria was declared a republic for the first time, with Salzburg as a *Bundesland*.

In 1920, the first Salzburg Festival opened on the steps of the cathedral with the performance of *Jedermann (Everyman)*. The festival was founded by many individuals, but notably the theatre director Max Reinhardt, the composer Richard Strauss and Hugo von Hofmannsthal, one of Austria's most renowned poets and lyricists. Its primary aim was to bring great music to the people with little or no influence from commercial contributions. In theory, this aim has been maintained, although today ticket prices range from just affordable to outrageously expensive. The festival was at its height from 1920 to 1938, growing in international stature every year.

With the annexation of Austria by Germany in 1938 (*Anschluss*) things changed. Many of the musicians, singers and conductors, who had helped make the festival

Festival founder

Max Reinhardt (1873–1943) was one of the co-founders of the Salzburg Festival. Born in Baden near Vienna in 1873, he was forced into exile in the US in 1938. He was also the founder of the Max-Reinhardt-Seminar at the University of Vienna, a drama college that runs four-year acting courses.

what it was, were Jewish or had Jewish relatives. They were not allowed to perform. Before taking over the running of the festival, the Nazi Party accused the Jews and clerics of misusing the festival idea. Max Reinhardt fled the country for England and then the US in 1938. Artur Toscanini, who had conducted many performances prior to the arrival of fascism, had left the country a year previously to conduct in the US. The festival continued in a diminished form with many performances only being held for army personnel until 1944. In 1947, it was relaunched under the patronage of the US Army. The festival flourished once again and was transformed into today's world-famous international music event that takes place every late July and August.

Salzburg Festival impresario, Max Reinhardt

World War II and Beyond

During World War II, Salzburg again escaped the worst of the horrors. For the first few years of the war, life continued much as it had before. It was only the large number of refugees from bombed cities in Germany that reminded the population that they were at war. But from autumn 1944 to the spring of 1945, a number of American bombing raids took place, killing 547 people.

The Americans were trying to destroy supply lines by targeting the railway tracks, but bombs caused much damage to the old parts of the town, including the cathedral, which suffered a direct hit. In May 1945, American troops entered the city and the war was over for the Salzburgers.

After hostilities ceased, the US Army oversaw Salzburg's post-war reconstruction. In 1955, the occupying troops left Austria and a new republic was declared. There followed a huge amount of construction work; the Festival Halls were built and also many new high-rise buildings and housing estates, so that the city expanded considerably. The university and the cathedral were also rebuilt and, in 1967, a preservation order was placed on the Old Town.

Austria joined the EU in 1995 and the European Monetary Union in 1999. In 2002, the euro replaced the Austrian schilling as the official currency. With the open border between Germany and Austria, the number of tourists coming to Salzburg has increased dramatically over recent decades. The airport has been enlarged a number of times to cope with the influx of mainly British charter flights in winter, and now also the many flights from Russia and Scandinavia. The city was placed on the Unesco World Cultural Heritage Site listing, which has attracted yet more visitors. In preparation for the year-long celebration of Mozart's birth in 2006, the city made sure all its sights were looking their best, and many of the buildings have been restored, renovated or rebuilt over the past few years.

Crowds gather at the Salzburg Festival Halls

Historical Landmarks

4000BC Stone Age settlement on Rainberg.

1000BC Illyrian settlement.

500BC The Celts invade the region and settle; salt mining begins.

15BC The Romans conquer the region; Juvavum (Salzburg) emerges.

470 St Severin founds a monastic settlement at Salzburg.

696 Bishop Rupert of Worms is given the city of Salzburg.

c.700 St Peter's Abbey and Nonnberg Convent are founded by Rupert.

739 Salzburg becomes a bishopric and later an archbishopric.

8th century First cathedral built by St Virgil.

1077 Archbishop Gebhard commissions Hohensalzburg fortress.

1167 Frederick Barbarossa burns the city to the ground.

1348–9 Salzburg is struck by plague; a third of the population dies.

16th century Peasants' War.

16th–17th century Archbishops Wolf Dietrich von Raitenau, Markus Sittikus and Paris Graf von Lodron give the city its modern-day appearance.

1623 University founded by Archbishop Paris Graf von Lodron.

1756 Wolfgang Amadeus Mozart born at Getreidegasse 9.

1781 Mozart moves to Vienna after arguing with the archbishop.

1800 French troops march into Salzburg.

1816 Salzburg becomes part of the Austro-Hungarian Empire.

1861 First elected parliament and provincial government in Salzburg.

1917 Salzburg Festival Hall Association founded.

1920 Salzburg becomes a province of the Democratic Republic of Austria. First Salzburg Festival takes place.

1938 German troops march into Austria.

1945 US troops enter the city.

1956–60 Building of the Large Festival Hall.

1962 Paris Lodron University Salzburg reopens.

1967 Easter Festival founded. Old Town preserved by law.

1997 Old Town of Salzburg becomes a World Cultural Heritage Site.

2006 Salzburg celebrates 250th anniversary of Mozart's birth.

2008 100th anniversary of Herbert von Karajan's birth.

WHERE TO GO

Although in tourist terms, Salzburg is geared towards everything Mozart, the city also offers a multitude of fascinating historical sights. There are ample churches, graveyards, gardens and alleyways dating back to medieval times. Salzburg is divided into an Old Town and a New Town, on opposite sides of the Salzach, and this chapter has been divided into areas of interest on both sides of the river, followed by a number of excursions. Depending on how much time you have, a walking tour is recommended to fully appreciate all that Salzburg has to offer *(see page 116)*. As the exact opening times for some of the sights vary from year to year, you might want to check with the Tourist Information Office on Mozartplatz on arrival.

For the sights such as the zoo, the Untersberg and Hellbrunn Palace, you can take a bus from the railway station or Hanuschplatz. Hallein and Werfen can be reached by train from the railway station. A bus will take you to the Salzkammergut lake district *(see page 77)*, but the area is better appreciated if you hire a car. You can also visit the Grossglockner Road and the Krimml Waterfalls by car or on an organised excursion.

THE MÖNCHSBERG AND ENVIRONS

The great **Mönchsberg** rock which towers over the Old Town provides Salzburg with a spectacular backdrop of white cliffs. Some of the earliest people in the area settled on this mountain as it provided a natural defence against predators and invaders from nearby territories. A walk across the Mönchsberg's ridge, strewn with old battlements and crumbling walls, provides today's visitors with panoramic and tree-framed views of

Snow-dusted rooftops of Salzburg's Old Town

Salzburg and is an excellent introduction to the city's main sights. Below the eastern ridge is the Old Town, with the palaces and squares of the Prince-Archbishops' quarter and the cathedral's green domes. Further to the northeast, across the Salzach River, is the New Town, built in the shadow of the Kapuzinerberg. The Mönchsberg's western ridge looks out across the suburbs to the distant Untersberg.

If you don't mind quite a steep uphill walk, there are many pedestrian routes up the Mönchsberg apart from the funicular train on Festungsgasse. A lift on Gstättengasse allows easy access to the Museum of Modern Art *(see page 48)*.

The Festung Hohensalzburg
On top of the Mönchsberg sits the magnificent fortress, the **Festung Hohensalzburg** (open daily Jan–Apr and Oct–Dec 9.30am–5pm, May–June, Sept, Easter and weekends in Dec

The Festung Hohensalzburg

9am–6pm, July–Aug 9am–7pm; admission fee includes museums and access to the external parts of the fortress; for an additional fee a guided tour or a solo audioguide tour allows access to other internal rooms; tel: 8424 3011).

In the grounds of the fortress

The Hohensalzburg is the largest and best preserved fortress in Europe, its dominating bastions, walls and towers making it the symbol of Salzburg. It has had a fascinating history under its many ruling archbishops. Construction began in 1077 under the reign of Archbishop Gebhard and it was enlarged and renovated up until the 17th century. Its late gothic appearance is largely due to the building work of the 15th-century archbishop Leonhard von Keutschach (1495–1519), who was not only a religious leader but also, like many archbishops, a powerful temporal ruler. He thus needed constant protection from outside invasion and even revolts from within his own territories. During this period, the main building of the fortress was significantly enlarged. There is a marble memorial to von Keutschach on the wall of St George's Church, and he is also commemorated by numerous insignia and coats of arms that include his curious personal symbol, seen by some as a turnip, by others as a beetroot. Since von Keutschach's time, the lion that is the symbol of the fortress has held a turnip (or beetroot) in its paws.

The Hohensalzburg was more than just a defensive fortress and residence in war-torn times. During periods when there was no direct military threat to the city, it was used as

Hangman's House

If you take the fortress tour up to the Reck watchtower, you will be rewarded with a spectacular view of the city and beyond. The white house in the middle of the open green space to the southwest is known as the Hangman's House. It is said that such was the desire of the citizens not to live next to the city's hangman that he was obliged to live alone in this isolated location.

a barracks and a prison. Archbishop Wolf Dietrich von Raitenau was held prisoner there by his nephew and successor, Markus Sittikus, for five years until his death in 1617.

The rich and lavishly decorated interior of the fortress is a breathtaking display of intricate gothic wood carvings and ornamental paintings. Two rooms not to be missed are the **Golden Chamber**, which features stunning detailed wood ornamentation and a majolica ceramic oven from the 1500s, and the **Golden Hall**, with its magnificent wood panelling and carving, and a fascinating ceiling supported by large twisted pillars.

One unique exhibit is the **Salzburger Stier** (Salzburg Bull), possibly the oldest working barrel organ in the world, built in 1502 and lovingly restored, which roars out melodies by Mozart and Haydn.

The fortress contains no less than three museums, which span a variety of topics and can only be seen after an officially conducted tour of the fortress. The **Rainer-Regiments-Museum** is full of military paraphernalia recalling the Imperial and Royal Regiment of Archduke Rainer; the **Fortress Museum**, renovated in 2000, has medieval art, weapons, instruments of torture and a variety of everyday objects that illuminate the history of the fortress and its occupants; and the **Marionettenmuseum** in the cellars of the fortress captures the spirit of the famous Salzburg Marionette Theatre with a display of historical puppets.

If you do not have time to enjoy the splendour of the interior, the courtyard offers some more historical sights, such as the old lime tree, said to be several hundred years old, and the fortress well, which dates from 1539. Even if you're not particularly interested in ancient fortresses, Hohensalzburg is worth a visit just for the views. From the Reck watchtower, you get a panoramic sweep of the Alps, and the Kuenberg bastion offers a fine view of Salzburg's domes and towers.

Nonnberg Convent

Nonnberg Convent

On the southeastern side of the Mönchsberg, to the east of the Hohensalzburg Fortress, is the **Nonnberg Benedictine Convent** (open daily 7am–dusk; closed during Mass), which is the oldest convent north of the Alps. As with many buildings in Salzburg, fire destroyed the original and what we see today is a gothic-style convent from the 1400s, though extensive renovations were done in 1895 and 1951.

The convent was founded in c.700 by St Rupert, who promptly appointed his niece,

Winged altar, St John's Chapel

St Erentrudis, as the first abbess. The founding patron of the romanesque church, Henry II, built a basilica here in 1009, and the 12th-century frescoes are some of the most impressive wall paintings in Austria. The church was severely damaged by fire in 1423. In 1464, the abbess, Agatha von Haunsberg, began the reconstruction in a gothic style, creating the unique crypt and the magnificent reticulate rib-vaulting. The tomb of St Erentrudis is located in the apse and most of the frescoes are from the 12th century. There is also a tombstone for Maria Salome, daughter of Archbishop Wolf Dietrich and his mistress, Salome Alt. In the nuns' choir there is a winged altar with a central shrine revealing the Madonna between the two patron saints, Rupert and Virgil.

St John's Chapel (near the entrance) features a gothic winged altar from the late 1400s. The four figures on the south door pay homage to St Erentrudis, the Virgin Mary, St Rupert and Emperor Henry II. The convent is full of interesting artefacts, though visitors are only allowed into the church and St John's Chapel (ask for the key at the convent entrance).

The Sound of Music footnote: in 1927 the real-life Maria von Kutschera and Baron von Trapp were married at Nonnberg Convent. Maria had been a postulant here in 1924.

Nonntal District

If you walk around the convent building and along the Nonn-berggasse you will eventually come out at Brunnhausgasse. Follow this road to the right and you will get to the **Leopolds-kron** district *(see page 58)*, while heading left you will short-ly reach the quiet **Nonntaler Hauptstrasse**. Situated here is the Erhardplatz, which sits in front of the church of **St Er-hard im Nonntal**. Built in 1685 by the architect Johann Cas-par Zuccalli, it has a richly decorated interior of stucco and a high altar painting by Johann Michael Rottmayr from 1692.

Below the Nonnberg Convent to the north is **Kajetaner-platz**, whose notable feature is the church of **St Kajetan**. It was consecrated in 1700 and only properly finished after 1730, based on plans by Johann Zuccalli. The portrait of the Holy Family on the left side altar is by Johann Michael Rottmayr; all the other altar paintings and the ceiling fresco are the work of Paul Troger. The Holy Staircase (1712), to the left of the main body of the church, is based on the Scala Santa in Rome.

Leading off Kajetanerplatz is the quiet shopping street of **Kaigasse**, which is lined with shops, galleries and cof-fee houses. Most of these buildings were once the homes of priests. On Chiemseegasse, off Kaigasse, is an even more elevated ecclesiastical residence, the **Chiemseehof**. From the 14th century, this was the seat and residence of the bishops of Chiemsee in Bavaria, a filial diocese of Salzburg. The Chiemseehof is not open to visitors, as it now houses the province of Salzburg's regional parlia-ment (Salzburger Landtag) and government (Salzburger Landesregierung).

Salzburg's signs

Salzburg is full of signs and insignias carved into walls and doorways. If you see 'C+M+B' and a year writ-ten in chalk above a door, this means that the carol-singers have been to the house and received a dona-tion for charity that year.

A view from the Festung Hohensalzburg across the Old Town

THE OLD TOWN

The **Altstadt** (Old Town), is a combination of tall merchants' houses and narrow alleys, along with the Baroque buildings and squares of the Prince-Archbishops' quarter. The area is compact and easily accessible on foot as most of it is a designated pedestrian zone.

St Peter's Abbey

Below the fortress, at the foot of the Mönchsberg, is the peaceful complex of **St Peter's Abbey**, the oldest active monastery in Austria. Founded in c.700 by St Rupert, a Frankish missionary, St Peter's is recognised as the spiritual centre around which Salzburg grew. Having been destroyed by fire in 1127 and thereafter subjected to many alterations, the **church** shows traces of several architectural styles. Its romanesque tower, for instance, is topped by a Baroque cupola. Similarly, the interior is high romanesque, but the altars are definitively in the rococo style. Most of the altar paintings are by Martin Johann Schmidt, and show his characteristic style with its contrasts of light and dark. There is also a plaque dedicated to Nannerl, Mozart's sister, and a memorial to the composer Johann Michael Haydn, the younger brother of the more famous Franz Joseph.

St Peter's bore witness to the music of 13-year-old Mozart in 1769: he wrote his *Dominicus Mass* (K66) for the first Mass officiated here by his childhood friend Kajetan Rupert Hagenauer, later the abbot of St Peter's. In 1783, Mozart's *Mass in C Minor* (K427) was first performed here under the direction of the composer, with his new wife Constanze singing the soprano part.

The church's **cemetery** is sprinkled with beautiful wrought-iron grave markers. This is the final resting place of many of Salzburg's aristocracy, and also of Nannerl Mozart, who died in October 1829. Bordering the cemetery are the famous **catacombs** (open May–Sept Tue–Sun 10.30am–5pm, Oct–Apr Wed–Thur 10.30am–3.30pm, Fri–Sun 10.30am–4pm; admission fee). These were carved into the wall of the rock during early Christian times and emanate a spiritual eeriness.

Cemetery at St Peter's church

On the right, next to the church, is **St Peter's Stifts-keller** (open daily 11am–midnight), a wine tavern since 803 and nowadays a traditional restaurant complex where you can enjoy the finest *Salzburger Nockerl* in town *(see page 94)* and the fantastic Mozart Dinner *(see page 87)*.

Kapitelplatz

If you leave St Peter's by the cemetery exit, you will find yourself in **Kapitelplatz**, which is easily recognisable by the massive chess board on the ground. You can always catch a good game here and watch as locals and tourists try to out-wit each other. Also on Kapitelplatz is **Neptune's Fountain**, built in 1732 by the sculptor Anton Pfaffinger on the site of one of the horse ponds during the rule of Archbishop Leopold Anton Firmian. During the summer months, Kapitelplatz is host to markets, sports events and many artists and musicians. On the far south side of the square, you will find the entrance to the Festungsgasse, which is the road up to the fortress and home to the **Stieglkeller** (open daily 10am–11pm), a classic pub with a live band every evening. The Festungsgasse also provides views of the city that you may recognise from *The Sound of Music*.

Stalls on Kapitelplatz

The Cathedral

Stepping through the north-ernmost arches of Kapitel-platz brings you onto the **Domplatz**, home to Salz-burg's **cathedral** (open winter 6.30am–5pm, summer 6.30am–7pm). In the centre of the square is the statue of the Virgin Mary, a master-piece of the Hagenauer broth-ers, created in 1766. Each year, the opening of the Salzburg Festival is celebrated here with a performance of *Jedermann (Everyman)*.

Salzburg's cathedral

The cathedral, the most impressive Baroque edifice north of the Alps, is the ecclesiastical centre of Salzburg. The original cathedral on this site was built by Bishop Virgil in 767. It was destroyed by fire in 1167, and ten years later a new cathedral was built on a grander scale, only to be destroyed once again by fire in 1598. The then archbishop, Wolf Dietrich, demolished the remains and dug up the graveyard in order to start rebuilding from scratch. But his plans were never realised as he was imprisoned by his nephew and successor, Markus Sittikus, who commissioned Santino Solari to rebuild the cathedral to a different design. The building escaped damage during the Thirty Years' War and was consecrated with much pomp and ceremony. Much later, it suffered a third calamity during a bombing raid in 1944, when the dome was destroyed. The cathedral was re-consecrated in 1959 after renovations. At the gates of the cathedral you can see the dates of the three consecrations: 774, 1628 and 1959. The towering white statues at the cathedral gates depict the patron saints Rupert and Virgil (outside) and the two apostles Peter and Paul (inside).

The cathedral's interior dates mostly from the 17th century. The only earlier survival is the 1321 font, supported by four even older 12th-century lions, where Mozart was baptised. One of the most impressive items in the cathedral is the massive and majestic organ, which is guarded by carved angels.

In the cathedral's magnificent Baroque oratories is the **Cathedral Museum** (open mid-May–Oct and late Nov–early Jan Mon–Sat 10am–5pm, Sun 11am–6pm; admission fee), which displays artefacts spanning its 1,300-year history, including medieval sculptures, Baroque paintings and gold articles from the cathedral treasury. The oldest exhibit is St Rupert's 8th-century crozier. There are also natural history objects and curiosities including fossils, gems and carved ivory.

In the **crypt**, traces of the old romanesque cathedral have been unearthed. The cathedral excavations (open July–Aug daily 9am–5pm; admission fee), revealing ruins of the original foundations, are entered around the corner on Residenzplatz, left of the main entrance. Other artefacts from the excavations form part of the Salzburg Museum's collection *(see page 40)*.

Johann Michael Rottmayr

Johann Michael Rottmayr (1654–1730) was a renowned Baroque artist, born in Laufen, Salzburg Province, whose style was influenced by the Venetian art of painting in the 16th century. His speciality was ceiling frescoes – he designed and executed most of those in the Salzburg Residenz and also in the Viennese Winter Riding School. He designed the altar in the Universitätskirche in Salzburg and the original painting *The Apotheosis of St Charles Borromeo* (the intercessor for people stricken with the plague), which can be seen in the Residenz Gallery.

Residenzplatz

Leaving Domplatz through the archways will bring you to **Residenzplatz**, Old Town's largest square. It is used for seasonal markets and events, though one stunning constant is the **Residenz Fountain**, created by Tommaso di Garona between 1656 and 1661. The fountain is 15m (50ft) high and is said to be the largest and most beautiful Baroque fountain outside Italy. If you are visiting in wintertime, though, you will find it covered up for protection against the elements.

The imposing Residenz Fountain

The **Residenz** (open daily 10am–5pm, last entry at 4.30pm; closed on certain special occasions; admission fee) was the residence and seat of the prince archbishops. A bishop's residence had existed on this site since medieval times; the present building, an extensive complex enclosing three large courtyards, was built around the turn of the 17th century for Archbishop Wolf Dietrich von Raitenau.

The marble portal on Residenzplatz leads into the main courtyard. Take the staircase on the left up to the state rooms and apartments. Decorated in late Baroque style, the rooms feature fine wall and ceiling paintings by Johann Rottmayr and Martino Altomonte. As a member of the Salzburg court music ensemble, the young Mozart would regularly perform before invited guests in the Rittersaal

(Knights' Hall), which is still used as a concert venue today. On the third floor is the **Residenz Gallery** (open Tue–Sun 10am–5pm), where European paintings from the 16th to the 19th century are displayed.

East of the fountain is the **Neue Residenz** (New Residence), built by Archbishop Wolf Dietrich as a 'guest wing'. The state rooms inside (guided tours only; closed during special events) feature detailed arabesques, including the three Christian virtues, the four cardinal virtues and Wolf Dietrich's coat of arms. In 1695, the famous **Glockenspiel** was added by Prince Archbishop Johann Ernst von Thun. Each day at 7am, 11am and 6pm, the 35 bells ring out across the city, with the tunes changing according to the season.

Entering the Residenz

The Neue Residenz (entrance at Mozartplatz 1) is home to the new **Salzburg Museum**, which opened in 2007 (open Tue–Sun 9am–5pm, Thur until 8pm, July–Aug and Dec also Mon 9am–5pm; admission fee). The collection features art and artefacts from all periods of Salzburg's history, ranging from prehistoric objects, such as a Celtic beaked pitcher and a Bronze-Age helmet, to a set of early 19th-century romantic paintings of the city. Temporary exhibits will focus on local personalities, artists, photographers, writers, musicians and scientists.

Mozartplatz

Next to Residenzplatz is **Mozartplatz**, a square dominated by a statue of Salzburg's favourite son. The disappointingly small bronze statue of Mozart was unveiled on 5 September 1842 as the composer's two sons looked on. His widow Constanze had died in March of that year, and at Mozartplatz No. 8 you will find a plaque dedicated to her memory. The statue, originally scheduled to be unveiled in 1841, had been delayed for a year because a Roman mosaic floor was discovered on the site during the preparations for its installation.

Monumental Mozart

A Controversial Statue

Right from the start, the statue of Mozart in Mozartplatz has been the cause of controversy. Intended to commemorate the 50th anniversary of Mozart's death, the statue was eventually unveiled a year late, at the 51st anniversary. As part of the unveiling ceremony, Mozart's son, a minor composer and musician, performed only a few of his father's works before moving on to play some of his own compositions. He was soon dismissed from the stage.

As for the statue itself, by all accounts it is not a very good likeness. And it includes a glaring anachronism. The composer is portrayed holding a pencil in his hand, even though pencils were not invented until 20 or 30 years after his death. Mozart would have written with a quill pen.

Alter Markt

There are two main exits leading off Mozartplatz. To the east is Kaigasse, which is part of the Nonntal district *(see page 33)*. To the west is **Judengasse**, home to the Jews of Salzburg until they were expelled from the city in 1498. This cobbled pedestrian street scores highly for charm and unusual shops, including a Christmas Shop, where you can buy yuletide decorations all year round, and a shop selling beautifully decorated eggs for use as Easter decorations.

Judengasse ends as you reach **Alter Markt**, another of Salzburg's busy squares. Besides the impressive fountain that surrounds a statue of St Florian, you will also find the chemist, Hofapotheke, the oldest in Salzburg and still displaying its medicinal preparations in old brown vials. Just opposite the chemist, at No. 10A, is the smallest shop in Salzburg, formerly a residence. If you are thirsty at this stage,

Mozart merchandise in the Alter Markt

have a coffee in Café Tomaselli, which has been in the
Alter Markt since 1705.
During both winter and summer, you will find markets
and/or mulled wine stands in
Alter Markt.

Getreidegasse

Leading on from Judengasse,
west of Alter Markt, is Salzburg's most famous shop-
ping street, **Getreidegasse**.
Whether you like shopping
or not, you should have at
least one walk down this busy

Mozart's Birthplace

pedestrian street. One of the first things you will notice are the
skilfully crafted wrought-iron guild signs that hang above most
of the shops and give the street its special character. Also of
interest are the numerous passageways and courtyards leading off the Getreidegasse, notably the Schatz-Haus-Passage
which has an impressive relief of the Madonna and child and
enters onto Universitätsplatz. Looking up you may notice that
as the houses get taller, their windows get smaller, creating a
strange optical effect. There are shops here selling traditional
Loden clothes and others offering authentic Austrian food.

The Getreidegasse is also part of the pilgrimage trail for
Mozart fans: No. 9 is **Mozart's Birthplace**, the house where
he was born on 27 January 1756 and lived with his family
until 1773. The Mozarts' apartment on the third floor and the
rooms on the second floor have been transformed by Robert
Wilson into a museum with an extravagant twist (open daily
9am–6pm, July–Aug 9am–7pm; admission fee). On display
are manuscripts (facsimiles), documents and souvenirs, and

portraits of the family members, including *Mozart at the Piano*, an unfinished 1789 oil painting by Wolfgang's brother-in-law, Joseph Lange. Also here are instruments that were played by the great musician: his concert piano and clavichord, his concert and child's violin, and a viola.

All of the passageways leading off Getreidegasse to the south reach **Universitätsplatz** (University Square), which is home to the academic district and the **Collegiate Church** (open daily), one of Johann Bernhard Fischer von Erlach's finest achievements. The interior is immensely high and features an array of angels on stucco clouds surrounding the Madonna. Universitätsplatz is the site of the daily vegetable market, which is a bit on the expensive side.

Horse Pond and Fountain

Festival District

Just east of here on Herbert-von-Karajan-Platz is the picturesque **Pferdeschwemme** (Horse Pond and Fountain), which incorporates a stunning mural of horses. The fountain was built in 1695 to serve as the washing area for the prince archbishops' horses that were kept in stables next door.

This adjacent site along Hofstallgasse has latterly been occupied by the famous **Festspielhäuser** (Festival Halls, guided tours Jan–May and Oct–20 Dec 2pm, June and Sept 2pm and 3.30pm, July–Aug 9.30am, 2pm and

3.30pm; admission fee). This is where, each year in high summer, Salzburg plays host to one of the best known music festivals in the world, the Salzburger Festspiele. The festival is centred on the three main venues here, though other locations around the city are also used. Based around the old Riding School, which was built in 1693 to train the archbishop's caval-

The Felsenreitschule theatre

ry, the present Festival Halls still preserve the original façade of the Baroque horse stables. Nowadays, the **Felsenreitschule** (riding school) is a theatre with a retractable roof for open-air performances, hosting high calibre operas and dramas. Next to the Felsenreitschule is the **House for Mozart**. This, the former Small Festival Hall, has been completely rebuilt with dramatically increased capacity. Adjoining the Felsenreitschule on its other flank is the 2,177-seat **Grosses Festspielhaus** (Large Festival Hall), designed by the Austrian architect Clemens Holzmeister, built between 1956 and 1960 and inaugurated by the conductor Herbert von Karajan. Guided tours – the only way to see the Festival Halls – provide a fascinating insight into the world of theatre.

The eastern end of Hofstallgasse opens into Max-Reinhardt-Platz where the **Rupertinum** (open Tue–Sun 10am–6pm, Wed 10am–9pm; admission fee) houses an important art collection of 20th-century works. In 2004, the main collection was moved to the new Museum of Modern Art on the Mönchsberg *(see page 48)*.

East of the Rupertinum is Sigmund-Haffner-Gasse, where you will find the entrance to the **Franciscan Church**

Altar in the Franciscan Church

(open daily 6.30am–7.30pm; closed during Mass), an elegant combination of the Baroque, romantic and gothic styles. A church was originally built here in the 8th century, but the city fire of 1167 destroyed all but the nave. Rebuilding around this core soon commenced and the building was consecrated in 1223. More additions followed, and the church was finally completed in 1460 by Stephan Krumenauer. Originally a part of St Peter's Abbey, it was handed over to the Franciscans by Archbishop Wolf Dietrich. Definitely worth a look is the high altar by Johann Bernhard Fischer von Erlach and the gothic statue of the Virgin Mary by Michael Pacher.

Around Gstättengasse

At the northeastern side of the Mönchsberg *(see page 27)* is the **Gstättengasse** where old houses are snugly built into the rock of the hill. In 1669, a rockfall killed 220 people, which is why there are rock cleaners whose job it is to scale the vertical rocks after the snows have melted to chip away at any loose stones or potential hazards.

At the northern end of Gstättengasse, you will find **Ursulinenplatz**, the site of another **Mozart statue**, erected in 2005 in anticipation of the 250th anniversary of Mozart's birth the following year. If modern sculpture does not appeal, you can also visit the former Ursuline Chapel that is now called **St Mark's Church** (Markuskirche). After the original chapel was destroyed by the 1669 rockfall, it was rebuilt and completed in 1705 by the architect Johann Bernhard Fischer von Erlach, who had to accommodate his design to suit the complicated wedge shape of the site.

Around the corner at Museumsplatz is the **Haus der Natur**, Salzburg's Natural History Museum (open daily 9am–5pm; admission fee). As well as the usual stuffed specimens, it has an impressive collection of live reptiles and a 36-tank aquarium. Besides wildlife, there are also mineral and geology displays and the Space Research Hall, with a life-size diorama of man's first steps on the moon. The museum also stages exhibitions and has a lovely terrace café.

Directly opposite the Haus der Natur is the former site of the Carolino Augusteum Museum, now relocated in the Neue Residenz on Mozartplatz under the name of Salzburg Museum *(see page 40)*.

African wildlife at the Natural History Museum

Just past the southern end of Gstättengasse is the **Church of St Blasius**, one of the oldest Gothic hall churches in existence (1330–50). The former civic hospital adjacent houses the **Spielzeugmuseum** (Toy Museum; open daily 9am–5pm; admission fee). Displayed here are all kinds of old toys – such as dolls' houses, miniature trains and railways, optical illusions, musical instruments and paper theatres – giving a fascinating insight into the childhood pleasures of times past.

Museum of Modern Art

A lift at Gstättengasse 13 allows access to the top of the Mönchsberg, where you will find the **Museum der Moderne** (Museum of Modern Art; open Tue–Sun 10am–6pm, Wed 10am–9pm; daily during festivals; admission fee). Straight lines, shimmering glass and bright white stone create a stark minimalist edifice which dominates the northwestern ridge of

The minimalist Museum of Modern Art

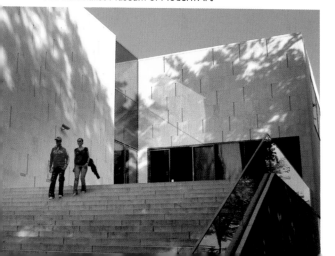

the Mönchsberg, 60m (200ft) above the city. Built on the site of the old Café Winkler, which crowned the plateau for many decades, the new building, designed by Friedrich Hoff Zwink and opened in 2004, respectfully incorporates the old tower into its new structure. The four levels of bright white Untersberg marble are designed to accommodate an ever-changing and diverse range of exhibitions, plus a permanent collection of works by Klimt, Kokoschka and other, lesser-known artists. The glass ceilings and the use of stairways as natural light shafts adds to the viewing pleasure. If you are feeling peckish and have some cash to spare, then try out the Mönchsberg 32 restaurant, which offers one of the best panoramic views of the city. The museum can also be reached by walking along the Mönchsberg from the fortress (see pages 27–8).

Mülln

North of the Mönchsberg is the **Mülln** district of Salzburg. This neighbourhood is home to a celebrated brewery run by monks, **Augustinerbräu** (open Mon–Fri 3–11pm, Sat–Sun 2.30–11pm). Visitors can enjoy the strong brown ale in a grand and delightfully traditional tavern, where the large beer garden is a great place to meet locals and tourists during the summer months.

The brewery and tavern at the Mülln Monastery have been in existence since 1621, hence the unique taste of the beer, which is brewed using traditional, old-fashioned methods. The monastery, built on the northern slopes of the Mönchsberg between 1607 and 1614, was founded by monks of the Augustine order, who were called to Salzburg from Bavaria by Archbishop Wolf Dietrich. When the monks began to dwindle in number during the 19th century, the monastery was handed over to the Benedictines from Michaelbeuern. It is now the parish church of Mülln. The interior dates from 1738 and has magnificent examples of delicate Baroque detail.

THE NEW TOWN

Linzergasse

The Staatsbrücke (State Bridge) over the Salzach leads to the new side of town – though it's only new in comparison with its ancient counterpart across the river. Walking directly over the bridge you will come to the **Linzergasse**, which brims with historical sights and stories. Many of the old houses were built during the 14th and 15th centuries, though a devastating fire in 1818 caused serious damage to the north side of the river. The Linzergasse was rebuilt and several of the old burgher houses were renovated and still line the street today. The house at No. 3 was the residence of the natural scientist Paracelsus (Theophratus Bombastus von Hohenheim), who lived here between 1540 and 1541. On the wall of the Hotel Gablerbräu is a plaque dedicated to the operatic baritone Richard Mayr, who was born here in 1877.

Looking across from the Old Town to the New

St Sebastian's Church

Just opposite the Gablerbräu is the grand entrance to the climb up the Kapuzinerberg, the hill that dominates the skyline on the north side of town *(see page 57)*. Slightly further up the Linzergasse is the entrance to the **Church**

of St Sebastian. The original Gothic church was built between 1505 and 1512 by Archbishop Leonhard von Keutschach. Deteriorating over the years, it was torn down in 1750 and replaced with a Baroque hall. The town fire of 1818 destroyed parts of the church, most regrettably the ceiling frescoes and high altar painting. The church was renovated again in 1820 (only the 1752 rococo doorway remains from the former church building),

St Sebastian's Church

and more restoration work was completed in 1996.

Definitely worth a visit is the adjoining **cemetery** (open summer 9am–7pm, winter 9am–4pm), which is surrounded by four arcades, and scattered with tombs, shrines and holy relics. Built by Archbishop Wolf Dietrich, the cemetery is dominated by the **Chapel of St Gabriel** in the centre, which contains his mausoleum. The chapel has a remarkable interior: the walls are clad with tiny coloured ceramic tiles, which contrast dramatically with the brilliant white stucco. The surrounding cemetery is the final resting place of many of Salzburg's best-known names, including Paracelsus, Mozart's widow Constanze and his father Leopold.

Makartplatz

A short walk northwest from the Staatsbrücke brings you to **Makartplatz**, dominated by the awesome Church of the Holy Trinity, which was built between 1694 and 1702. No. 9 Makartplatz is **Mozart's Residence**, where the Mozart family lived from 1773 to 1780. The house does not offer much in terms of architectural beauty. It did, however, offer exactly what Leopold Mozart wanted: more space than their former home on the Getreidegasse for the family to live and especially for Wolfgang to work. Indeed, Mozart produced many symphonies, concertos, arias, masses and other sacred music in this house. After he had flown the nest, his mother had died and his sister had married, only Leopold remained in the house.

After Leopold died in 1787, the house had many owners. It was only in 1989 that the International Mozarteum Foundation was able to purchase the building, which had been rebuilt as an office block after a bomb struck it in 1944. In 1994, the Foundation tore down the office building and began rebuilding according to the original plans of the house. Today it is a museum that displays exhibits from the Mozart family and old musical instruments (open daily

The Mozarteum

In 1848, the International Mozarteum Foundation was formed to 'perform and propagate Mozart's music'. Today, the Foundation runs two museums in the city. Its collections include the composer's original letters and sheet music and numerous performances of his work.

The Foundation is best known for its two long-running concert series. Mozart Week (*Mozartwoche*) is held in late January, with a 10-day presentation of the composer's works to mark his birthday on 27 January. Performances often include concerts by the Vienna Philharmonic Orchestra and concertos by star pianists. In summer, the Foundation's concert series forms a key part of the Salzburg Festival (*see page 84*).

For Mozart Week information and tickets, contact the Mozarteum Foundation's Ticket Office at Theatergasse 2 (tel: 873 154; <www.mozarteum.at>). For Salzburg Festival schedules and tickets, visit the festival website at <www.salzburgfestival.at>.

9am–6pm, July–Aug until 7pm; may be closed in Mozart Week in Jan; admission fee).

Opposite Mozart's family house is the Landestheater (Regional Theatre) and, behind it, the Marionettentheater (Puppet Theatre) and the Mozarteum, making this area one of the artistic centres of the city. Built in 1892, the **Landestheater** is the centre of Salzburg's cultural programme, giving performances of all kinds throughout the year, including ballet and opera.

Performances in the **Marionettentheater** (Puppet Theatre) often include full operas enacted by the diminutive wooden characters. The theatre's puppeteers have travelled the world performing their classic operas and plays.

The **Mozarteum** is the headquarters of the foundation of the same name *(see box opposite)*, dedicated to the research and development of Mozart's music. The complex includes concert halls, recital rooms and a music school.

Concert hall in the Mozarteum

Mirabell Palace and Gardens

Next to the Landestheater is the entrance to the **Mirabell Gardens**, comprising geometrically designed flowerbeds, fountains, an orangery, a rose garden and lawns adorned with sculptures based on classical mythology. In *The Sound of Music*, this was where Maria and the children danced around the statue of Pegasus singing *Do Re Mi*. On the west side of the parterre is an open-air theatre, with trimmed hedges marking the wings and entrances, and next to it a garden housing marble dwarfs. Also in the gardens is the **Salzburger Barockmuseum** (Baroque Museum; open Wed–Sun 10am–5pm, July–Aug, Easter and Christmas Tue–Sun 10am–5pm; admission fee), which houses an important collection of 17th- and 18th-century oil sketches, drawings and sculpture models, with works by Giordano, Rottmayr, Bernini, Straub and others. There are plans for a museum of *The Sound of Music* to

In the manicured grounds of Mirabell Palace

be opened in 2009 in the same building.

The **Mirabell Palace** was built in 1606 by Archbishop Wolf Dietrich, who wanted a residence outside the town walls for his mistress Salome Alt and their children (of whom 10 survived infancy). The archbishop named the palace Altenau. After his imprisonment in the fortress and his death, his nephew and successor Markus Sittikus renamed the palace Mirabell in an attempt to conceal the blasphemous memory of its original purpose. Between 1721 and 1727, the palace was remodelled by Archbishop Franz Anton von Harrach. The stunning marble staircase is the work of Johann Lukas von Hildebrandt, with acrobatic cherubs added by the sculptor Georg Raphael Donner in 1726. The richly adorned **marble hall**, where the Mozart family once performed, was at one time the dining room. Today it is used for concerts and is hugely popular as a wedding venue.

Salzburger Barockmuseum

In 1818, the Mirabell was badly damaged in the great fire that ravaged the New Town. Fortunately the marble staircase and hall were undamaged. The current neoclassical style of the palace is thanks to Peter de Nobile, who was the court architect in Vienna and added the detailed work around the windows and the stuccowork.

Many well-known personalities have stayed at the palace, including Prince Otto of Bavaria, who later became the King of Greece, and the legendary Capuchin monk Joachim

Haspinger, who died in the palace in 1858. Today, the palace is the office of the Mayor of Salzburg *(Bürgmeister)* and the administration. That is why only certain parts of the building are open to the public (staircase daily 8am–6pm; marble hall Mon, Wed and Thur 8am–4pm, Tue and Fri 1–4pm).

Salzburg and *The Sound of Music*

Film lovers will recognise Salzburg and its environs as the setting for *The Sound of Music*. Most people know that the film was based on fact.

The central character, Maria, was born in 1905. A strict upbringing developed an antipathy towards religion in her. After a chance meeting with a priest, she changed her views and joined the Nonnberg Convent. To aid her recovery from an illness, she was sent as governess to the home of Georg von Trapp, a widower with seven children. Love blossomed, Maria and the captain were married in 1927, and had three children of their own. The von Trapp children were a musical bunch before Maria arrived, but she developed their skills further. When the Austrian Bank closed and Georg was suddenly penniless, the children began to sing to audiences for money. The von Trapps fled Austria in 1938.

Today, fans of the movie come here to retrace the big-screen von Trapp family's footsteps. The song *Do Re Mi* was sung in the Mirabell Gardens around the fountain. St Peter's Cemetery was reconstructed in the studios and used for the scene where the von Trapp family hide between tombstones while trying to escape the Nazis. The façade of Fohnburg Castle became the front of the von Trapp villa, while Leopoldskron Castle was the rear. The children go boating on the lake there and the ballroom was modelled on one of the rooms inside. The opening scenes in the convent were filmed at Nonnberg Abbey, the opening credit scenes around Lake Fuschl and the wedding at the church in Mondsee. The von Trapp family make their escape over the Untersberg, although in reality, this would not have been a wise move as it would have taken them straight to Hitler's Eagle's Nest *(see page 68)*.

Kapuzinerberg

Opposite the Hotel Gabler-bräu on the Linzergasse is the entrance to the path that leads to the top of **Kapuzinerberg**, Salzburg's highest point at 636m (2,087ft). The hill was inhabited during Neolithic times, and the two settlements above the monastery have been dated to 1000BC.

The Stations of the Cross on Kapuzinerberg

On the walk up you pass the six Baroque **Stations of the Cross**, which were built between 1736 and 1744. Halfway up is the **Felix Gate**, dating from 1632, which offers the first panoramic view of the city. At this point there is another path called Imbergstiege, which takes you past St John's Chapel and meets up with another path at the *Kanzel* or pulpit, where you will be rewarded by the breathtaking views of the city. Not surprisingly, the forests and quiet location of the Kapuzinerberg make it a haven for wildlife, including deer and badgers.

One cannot climb the Kapuzinerberg without visiting the **Capuchin Monastery**, which was originally a military tower and fortification system erected by nervous archbishops during the Middle Ages. It was Archbishop Wolf Dietrich who called the Capuchin monks to Salzburg in 1594 and transformed the fortification into a monastery and church. The monastery is surrounded by a wall, which runs from the Felix Gate and straddles the western, southern and eastern slopes. The towering cross and bastion of the monastery are dominant features of the landscape, though the monastery itself

Stefan Zweig

An influential Austrian author, Stefan Zweig (1881–1942) lived in Salzburg between the two world wars. Much translated in the 1930s, Zweig's writings included short stories, novels, literary essays and biographies of Marie Antoinette and Maria Stuart notable for their use of psychoanalytical theories. Although of Jewish origin, he described himself as an 'accidental Jew'.

is very modest. The Gothic oak door of the inner portal is said to be a relic from the old Salzburg Cathedral. The interior of the monastery church is simple, befitting a life of devotion.

Kapuzinerberg 5 is the former residence of the writer Stefan Zweig, who chose the house for its tranquil location. Having lived in Salzburg since 1919, he fled Austria in 1934 following Hitler's rise to power. He first lived in England (in Bath and London) and then the US before moving to Brazil in 1941, where he and his wife both committed suicide because of their concern for the future of Europe. There is a memorial to Zweig next to the Capuchin Monastery.

SALZBURG'S ENVIRONS

Leopoldskron Lake and Palace

A short walk south from the Nonntal area of the Old Town takes you to the Leopoldskron district, which contains the lake and palace of the same name. The **Leopoldskron Palace** was built by Archbishop Firmian in 1736 in rococo style. The archbishops used the palace for centuries, but in the early 20th century, it was bought by Max Reinhardt, one of the founders of the Salzburg Festival. He had it totally renovated and had the gardens laid out in their present form. Now the property of an American institute, it is used for conferences and seminars but unfortunately is not open to the public. However, you can see the palace from the lakeside path, which provides a lovely walk at any time of year. In the summer, the swans are wonderful to watch and in winter, the Salzburgers love to use the lake for ice-skating and curling matches.

The lake and the house featured in the filming of *The Sound of Music*. The rear of the house was used as the von Trapp villa and the boating scene was filmed on the lake.

Hangar-7

If you are in the vicinity of the airport, it's worth paying a visit to **Hangar-7** (Wilhelm-Spazier-Strasse 7A; open daily 9am–10pm; free). This is one of Salzburg's newest sights. Completed in 2003, it was built to house a collection of vintage aircraft. The hangar is a glass and steel dome in the shape of an aircraft wing and constitutes one of the highlights of modern architecture in Salzburg. Situated on the eastern apron of

Inside the spectacular glass dome at Hangar-7

Salzburg's airport, there are two buildings. The first and largest is the hangar that is open to the public. Facing and mirroring it on a smaller scale is Hangar-8, the maintenance hangar.

The museum on the ground floor not only houses aircraft, but also Formula 1 racing cars from the Red Bull teams. During the summer months, many of the aircraft are at various air shows around Europe and may not all be on display. However, there are changing art exhibitions to view throughout the year. There is also a bar, a café and a top-class restaurant, Ikarus *(see page 141)*.

Stiegl's Brauwelt

Not far from the airport and Hangar-7 is **Stiegl's Brauwelt** (Stiegl's World of Brewing, Bräuhausstrasse 9; open daily Sept–June 10am–5pm, July–Aug 10am–7pm, last entry 6pm; admission fee). Stiegl, probably the favourite local brew in Salzburg, is served in many of the pubs and restaurants around town. The brewery has been here for over 500 years and is the oldest one that is privately owned in Austria.

Attached to the brewery is a museum housing the largest beer exhibition in the world. There is a display of brewing techniques, machinery and unusual equipment through the ages. On the tour, you are shown how beer is made from start to finish and, thankfully, at the end you have the chance to sample it too.

Hellbrunn Palace

A short bus ride (route No. 25) from the railway station takes you south to **Hellbrunn Palace and Gardens** (Schloss Hellbrunn; palace open end Mar, Apr and Oct 9am–4.30pm, May–June and Sept 9am–5.30pm, July–Aug 9am–10pm; admission fee; gardens open daily summer 6am–9pm, winter 6.30am–5pm; free). The palace was built between 1613 and 1615 as a hunting lodge and summer residence for Markus

Sittikus. Its architect, Santino Solari, was also the man responsible for the reconstruction of Salzburg Cathedral. The Hellbrunn Festival is held in the palace and gardens every August.

The palace itself is not very large, and the interior is no longer complete, but it's worth visiting to see the wonderful Italian murals in the banqueting hall and the adjoining music room in the octagonal pavilion. The palace's **trick fountains** also delight visitors. Markus Sittikus had these built to amuse himself and his guests (but particularly himself). The **Roman Theatre** has stone seats that spew out water without warning, so Sittikus' guests would be unexpectedly soaked (as visitors still are today). Funnily enough, this does not happen to the archbishop's chair at the top. There are also many charming grottoes featuring similar watery surprises based on mythological themes. If you are carrying expensive camera equipment, make sure you are ready to cover it up quickly.

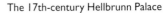

The 17th-century Hellbrunn Palace

Hydraulics also drive a large **mechanical theatre**, with moving figures and an organ that runs on water power.

The park area surrounding the palace dates from 1730, although some of its sculptures are from the early 17th century and include a statue of Empress Elisabeth. The pavilion that was used in *The Sound of Music* was relocated here from its original place at Leopoldskron.

Also in the grounds, about a 20-minute walk from the palace, is the **Stone Theatre**, formed by a natural gorge, where the first opera in the German-speaking world was presented in 1617.

Trompe l'oeil ceiling fresco in Hellbrunn Palace

On Hellbrunn Mountain, still inside the park, stands the Monatsschlössl (Month Castle), so-called because it was allegedly built in only one month. It houses a **Folklore Museum** (Volkskunde Museum; same opening hours as Hellbrunn Palace; admission fee), which displays costumes, masks, religious artefacts and agricultural equipment from the lively history of Salzburg.

Also on the mountain is **Salzburg Zoo** (open daily end Oct–end Mar 9am–4pm, end Mar–end Oct 9am–5pm, July–Aug until 6.30pm; admission fee). There has been a zoo on this site since 1421. Originally, it housed only alpine animals, but it has since been extended to include species from all over the world. Over 800 creatures can be seen here – many of them (no dangerous ones) allowed to roam freely around the grounds and beyond. There are often monkeys on the paths, storks in the nearby fields and vultures circling in the thermals above the Untersberg. In August, the zoo is open on Friday and Saturday evenings until 11pm (last entry 9.30pm) for 'Night Zoo' sessions, when the nocturnal animals are the star performers.

Klessheim Palace

The main part of **Klessheim Palace**, about 1.5km (1 mile) west of the city centre (No. 18 bus), was built by Austria's greatest Baroque architect, Johann Fischer von Erlach, for Archbishop Johann Ernst Thun between 1700 and 1709. He used designs and ideas from Versailles palace and gardens and eventually completed the construction in 1732. A panorama picture of Salzburg in 1829 is on view in the foyer.

It was used by the archbishops until Salzburg came under the control of the Habsburgs. In the late 19th century, Emperor Franz Josef banished his homosexual younger brother, Archduke Ludwig Viktor, to Klessheim Palace after Ludwig had

The *Föhn*

Situated so close to the Alps, Salzburg experiences a phenomenon called the *Föhn* for about 45 days of the year. A *Föhn* is created when air is forced up one side of a mountain range, causing it to expand and cool and lose its water vapour. When the dry air starts to move down the north side of the Alps, it warms as the pressure increases, creating strong, gusty, warm and dry winds. When a *Föhn* blows into Salzburg, it is enough to lay the whole city low. Headaches, asthma attacks and frayed nerves are common; the suicide rate, crime and traffic accidents increase. However, a *Föhn* day is generally a lovely day, bringing subtropical temperatures in summer and warm, pleasant days in winter.

Klessheim Palace

sparked a public scandal by making advances to an army officer in a swimming pool in Vienna. He died here in 1919.

Between 1938 and 1945, Hitler used the palace as his residence when he was in Salzburg. It was here that he met the Italian dictator Mussolini in 1940 and other heads of state from Hungary, Czechoslovakia and Romania. After the war, it became the headquarters of the occupying army. Then for a long time it was used by the provincial government to receive important state visitors such as Queen Elizabeth II.

Since 1993, it has housed the only year-round **casino** in Salzburg Province. You can enjoy the gardens and a few rooms of the palace free, but to enter the casino (open daily noon–3am) there is an admission fee which provides you with your first gaming chips. Minimum age for entry is 18 and you must provide some photo identification. As well as the No. 1 bus from the city centre, red-sided shuttle buses operated by the casino run from the foot of the Mönchsberg every hour from 11.30am to 11.30pm (returning hourly noon–midnight).

SOUTH OF SALZBURG

Untersberg

The highest mountain in the vicinity of Salzburg is the **Untersberg**, to the southwest. It can be seen for kilometres around as it juts up from the flatlands and towers 1,853m (6,078ft) above sea level. The mountain is a limestone massif with deposits of salt and marble. The terrain is craggy and steep, making it a strenuous climb on foot. If you do not have a car, you can take bus No. 25 to the bottom station of the cable car in **Grödig** (open daily July–Sept 8.30am–5.30pm, Mar–June and Oct 8.30am–5pm, Dec–Feb 9am–4pm). Alternatively, there is a cycle path that takes you all the way there. On a clear day, the views from the top are incredible. You can see the whole of the Salzburg basin, into Bavaria, the Watzmann (the second highest mountain in Germany) and as far as the Lake District (Salzkammergut) to the east and the Hohe Tauern mountains in the south. There are a few easy walks from the top station of the cable car to the viewpoints. For those who do not want to venture too far, there is a panoramic view from the top station.

Tucked beneath the northwest slopes of the Untersberg is the village of **Grossgmain**, which has an **Open-air Museum**

A view of the Untersberg from the Mönchsberg

(Freilicht Museum; open Easter–Oct Tue–Sun 9am–6pm, July–Aug daily, last entry 5pm; admission fee). The museum is one of the top attractions in the area and has won numerous awards. It includes a collection of old farmhouses that have been transferred from different parts of Salzburg Province and reconstructed with meticulous care. They span the last five centuries, showing how building and farming methods have changed and developed.

There are also many old farm machines to be viewed, and on Sundays and public holidays craftsmen demonstrate the old trades, from woodwork to bee-keeping, shoe-making to beer-brewing. The museum covers an area of 50 hectares (125 acres), so you will need a full day to see it all.

Legends of the Untersberg

According to legend, dwarfs, giants and wild virgins all live on the Untersberg. However, the mountain's main mythical character is Emperor Karl the Great, who is said to sleep within the mountain. Legend foretells a time when the ravens that circle the summit will stop and the Emperor's beard will have grown three times around a marble table. Then he will rise and fight the battle of good versus evil. The venue for this battle is quite specific: the pear tree in Wals. Once victorious, the Emperor will hang up his shield and an era of happiness and prosperity will follow. Other legends view the rising of the Emperor as Judgement Day, when the Antichrist will appear and do battle with angels.

Less portentously, historians debate the importance of the Untersberg during Celtic times, when Salzburg was geographically almost central in the Celtic empire. Given the pattern of early settlements found around Salzburg, it may be that the Untersberg was of great religious importance, and many of the mountain's legends have possible links with the political and religious propaganda of the early Middle Ages. Certainly few mountains in the Alps have generated such colourful mythology.

The snowcapped Watzmann seen from Berchtesgaden

Berchtesgaden

Just 30km (18 miles) south of Salzburg, across the border in Germany, is **Berchtesgaden**. Set amid beautiful alpine scenery dominated by the impressive peaks of Germany's second-highest mountain, the Watzmann (2,713m/8,900ft), this delightful little town encapsulates all the attractions of the Bavarian Alps, including painted houses, a little royal palace and wonderful views. But the area also has a dark side. The village of **Obersalzberg**, just above the town, was where in 1934 Hitler bought a chalet known as the Berghof (Mountain House), and had it decorated in the most pretentious style, with massive furniture, large rooms and heavy fireplaces. It became his country retreat, where he entertained his cronies, Nazi Party functionaries and, in 1938, Neville Chamberlain, the British prime minister. A Gestapo headquarters was established nearby, and beneath it all was a network of underground bunkers.

Most of these buildings, including the Berghof, were destroyed in an Allied air raid in 1945, and the remains were blown up by the West German government in 1953. But you can still visit the **Kehlsteinhaus** or **Eagle's Nest** – the 'teahouse' built by Martin Bormann as Hitler's 50th birthday present from the Nazi Party (open daily mid-May–Oct; inaccessible due to snow in winter; admission fee). It sits precariously on the top of Kehlstein mountain at 1,834m (6,017ft). If you have a car it has to be parked in Obersalzberg, where you can catch a bus to the summit, up a mountain road that was built specifically to reach the Eagle's Nest, a remarkable feat of engineering. Once at the top, you board the original brass-lined lift for the 124m (406ft) ascent to the house itself, which can be toured at leisure (though not all of it). The main teahouse area is now a restaurant and provides fantastic views, while some parts of the building are also used for conferences.

Also located in the Berchtesgaden area are the ancient **Salt Mines** (Salzbergwerk; open daily May–Oct 9am–5pm, Oct–Apr 11.30am–3pm; admission fee). Salt has been mined here since 1517, and still is today. Visitors are issued with old miners' clothing to take a tour of the mines, accompanied by a miner, starting in a small wagon on railway tracks. The rest of the tour includes sliding down a miners' chute and taking a ferry across an underground salt lake. One feature not to be missed is the 'chapel', a grotto of oddly shaped salt formations illuminated to eerie effect.

Königssee

To the south of Berchtesgaden, and within Germany's Berchtesgaden National Park, lies **Königssee**, one of the most beautiful lakes in the region. The narrow fjord-like lake runs 9km (5½ miles) north–south in the shadow of the Watzmann, its giant east face rising almost straight out of the water. There is a car park near the small village of Königsee, at the northern end of the 'fjord'. From here you can take a boat trip along the whole length of the lake. As only a small part of Königssee is visible from the village, the trip is highly recommended, to fully appreciate the stunning beauty of the scenery. There are two stops en route. The first is **St Bartholomä**, where there is a curious Baroque church with twin onion domes and a restaurant serving wonderfully fresh fish from the lake. The second is **Salet** at the lake's southern tip. The boat only goes this far in the summer months. There is a commentary on board in English about the lake's history, and the aims of the Berchtesgaden National Park. As the Königssee lies within a conservation area, every attempt is made to keep pollution levels down. The tourist boats are electric and, apart from rescue boats and farmers' boats, they are the only powered craft allowed on the lake.

A tranquil scene at Königssee

Hallein

About 15km (10 miles) south of Salzburg lies the busy little town of **Hallein**, the second largest town in Salzburg Province and the district capital of the Tennengau. You can reach it either by train or by car via the A10 Tauern motorway. Hallein has a delightful old town on the banks of the Salzach River. Most of the houses in the old town were built in the late Middle Ages, and many were renovated in the 1980s. Until the early 1990s, the town's Perner Island was an industrial site with a large salt processing plant, but it has now been turned into a cultural centre and every year stages a number of performances during the Salzburg Festival.

A large paper mill is the town's main employer, but in former years salt mining brought wealth to Hallein. Salt was discovered on the Dürrnberg by the Celts, and was mined there as recently as 1989. Now the mines are closed and have been turned into a museum. A tour of the **Dürrnberg Salt Mines** (Salzwelten Salzburg; guided tours daily, mid-Mar–Oct 9am–5pm, Nov–mid-Mar 10am–3pm; admission fee) demonstrates how salt was mined, explains the importance of salt and gives visitors the chance to go on an underground boat trip and a slide down an old miners' chute. Also included in the admission fee is the **Celtic Village**, a reconstruction of a village showing how the Celts lived and worked.

Back in the town itself, the biggest attraction is the **Celtic Museum** (open daily 9am–5pm; admission fee). It houses a collection of archaeological finds from

Dürrnberg Salt Mines

the area, including equipment used by the miners, as well as priceless burial offerings. The **Silent Night Museum** (open daily 3–5pm, Dec from 11am; admission fee) is a celebration of the famous Christmas carol whose composer, Franz Xaver Gruber, is buried in Hallein church cemetery. He was organist and choirmaster here after he left Oberndorf where he wrote the song.

Franz Xaver Gruber's grave

Werfen

If you continue south from Hallein along the A10 for another 29km (18 miles), you reach **Werfen**, a small market town situated on what was an important trade route for salt. The town is strung along a wide road and is pleasant to walk through. The parish church, built between 1652 and 1657, contains a very impressive Baroque altar and early Baroque side altars.

Castle Hohenwerfen (open Apr Tue–Sun 9am–4.30pm, May, June and Sept daily 9am–5pm, July–Aug daily 9am–6pm, Oct daily 9am–4.30pm; admission fee) was built in 1077 to guard the trade route. Frequent additions up to the 16th century have given it a fairytale appearance. It was used as a prison for many centuries and among those locked up there was Archbishop Wolf Dietrich von Raitenau in 1611. According to folklore, the dungeons in these castles were sometimes filled to capacity with innocent people, including

Protestant missionaries who had offended the archbishops of Salzburg in some way. It is said that these 'unwanted sorts' were locked up in darkness in solitary confinement for years and only set free after they had gone mad.

The castle **museum** has an armoury, and there are falconry displays twice a day, at 11am and 3pm. If the castle seems familiar to you, it may be because it was used in the 1968 film *Where Eagles Dare.*

Castle Hohenwerfen

Eisriesenwelt

The caves of **Eisriesenwelt** (World of the Ice Giants), east of Werfen, are the largest ice caves in Europe. They stretch for about 42km (26 miles), although only a fraction of that length is open to the public (guided tours daily May–Oct 9am–3.30pm; July–Aug until 4.30pm; admission fee includes cable car). Fantastic ice 'statues' and frozen waterfalls extend for about 1km (½ mile) from the entrance. The ice formations are created during the winter months when the water in the caves freezes, so the best time to see them is in the spring and early summer before the formations have started to melt again.

Drive or take a taxi-bus from Werfen's main square, then it's a 20-minute walk from the car park to the cable car station. In order to enter the caves, you have to take one of the many guided tours that start at regular intervals. As the temperature inside is always around freezing point, you must wear warm clothing – and sensible shoes to negotiate the narrow slippery passages. The caves are not recommended for the elderly, infirm or children. Although it's quite a strenuous excursion, it is certainly worth the effort.

The Grossglockner Road

One of the most spectacular scenic routes through the Alps is the **Grossglockner High Alpine Road**. The Grossglockner itself is Austria's highest mountain at 3,798m (12,460ft). It is situated in the Hohe Tauern range of mountains and in the national park of the same name, which straddles the provinces of Salzburg, East Tyrol and Carinthia.

The job of planning the road, running 48km (30 miles) between Bruck and Heiligenblut, was given to the engineer Franz Wallack in 1924. Construction started in 1930, taking five years. The road had to be rebuilt after World War II, having been seriously damaged by tank movements. Until the Felbertauern tunnel was built, this was the main road linking the provinces of Salzburg and Carinthia via the Alps. Since 1935, some 50 million people have made use of the road. It is popular with cyclists, motorcyclists – there are special facilities for parking motorbikes and equipment lockers along the route – car drivers and coach groups. On some sunny summer days, there can be thousands of people making the pilgrimage along this road.

Rural encounter

A toll road, it is officially open from the beginning of May until the end of October (open daily May–mid-June 6am–8pm, mid-June–mid-Aug 5am–10pm, mid-Aug–Oct 6am–7.30pm, last entry 45 mins before closing), but sometimes summer snowfalls can close it for days at a time. Before you set off, it's worth checking with the Ferleiten Information Point (tel: 06546 650) whether the road is actually open or not. The ticket you buy at the tollbooth gives you access to the road's exhibitions and sights.

There are various **viewpoints** to stop at along the way. The Fuscher Törl, which lies at 2,428m (7,966ft) above sea level, has a memorial built by Clemens Holzmeister to commemorate those who died during the construction of the road. The highest point of the through road is the Hochtor at 2,503m (8,212ft). You will be quite likely to find snow up here even in August. But if you take the detour to the Franz-Josefs-Höhe, which is highly recommended, you can get to an even higher point called the Edelweiss-spitze, at 2,571m (8,435ft).

You have the best view of the the Grossglockner itself from the Franz-Josefs-Höhe (2,369m/7,772ft), where there is a lift that takes you down to the Pasterze Glacier (note that the glacier is shrinking and so the bottom of the lift is now about 100m/100yds

The Grossglockner High Alpine Road

away from the start of the glacier). This is where you are most likely to see marmots lying in the sun. Access to walks and visitor centres are included in your ticket.

The road takes you through a variety of vegetation zones and is quite fascinating. There are also many activities to do with the family at places such as Fuscher Lake, at 2,262m (7,421ft), where there is an exhibition about the construction of the road. There is a geology path and, at Schöneck, a botanical path. Various restaurants are dotted along the route, but it is recommended to avoid lunchtimes at the Franz-Josefs-Höhe, as the restaurants there are very busy catering for the numerous coach parties.

Krimml Waterfalls

At the very western end of the Salzach Valley, just before the Gerlos road starts its steep ascent over the pass to the Tyrol, lie the **Krimml Waterfalls** (open daily mid-Apr–mid-Oct; admission fee; winter months no admission fee, but there is no guarantee that the path will be passable). Like the Grossglockner, they are part of the Hohe Tauern National Park. With a drop of 380m (1,247ft), the Krimmler Wasserfälle are the highest waterfalls in Europe and make a magnificent spectacle as they plunge down the mountainside in three stages. The falls are at their most impressive in the spring and early summer when the melt-waters turn the stream into a torrent. The Krimmler Ache starts at the Krimmler Kees glacier before plummeting down the falls.

The path up to the falls is relatively steep, but not difficult, and there are benches and viewpoints all along the route

Krimml Waterfalls in the Hohe Tauern National Park

where you can rest your legs while admiring the rainbow colours in the spray of the falls.

The first waterfall is 140m (460ft) high and the most spectacular of the three. This one can be viewed from the bottom without any strenuous walking. The walk from the car park will take around 10 minutes. From the bottom of the first falls to the second, which is 100m (330ft) high, will take half an hour. Then to the top falls (a 140m/460ft drop), it's another hour's climb. Allow plenty of time to get back before nightfall.

The falls have been popular with visitors for many years. The first rough steps to the top of the first falls were built in 1835. The existing path was completed in 1897, built by the local branch of the Alpine Club. For keen walkers there are several further trails that can be explored from the top of the falls.

Information panels at the bottom of the falls describe the flora and fauna in the area, as well as hydro-energy in *WasserWunderWelt* (The Wonderful World of Water).

THE SALZKAMMERGUT

The Salzkammergut (Salt Chamber Estate) refers to the wealth that salt brought to the region, but it is an area that today is more famous for its lakes and alpine scenery than for its salt industry, and is also known as the Lake District. The area extends from Fuschl near Salzburg to the Almtal in the east, with impressive peaks and more than 70 lakes. It is one of Austria's most popular tourist regions and often considered to be the jewel of the nation. The area has been popular with visitors since Emperor Franz Joseph spent his summers in Bad Ischl.

Fuschlsee

The first lake you come to heading east from Salzburg is **Fuschlsee**. About 25km (15 miles) from the city, it can be reached by the A1 motorway or along the B1/B158 (the

On the shore of Fuschlsee

prettier route). The lake is 4km (2½ miles) long and wonderfully warm in the summer. The steep, wooded slopes rising along its shore curve to its eastern shore where the village of Fuschl lies. This quiet little resort is popular with walkers in the summer and also offers watersports. If the countryside looks familiar, it may be that you recognise it from the opening titles of *The Sound of Music*, which was filmed here.

On the opposite shore, in its own extensive grounds, is Schloss Fuschl. This was originally a hunting lodge of the prince archbishops, then during World War II it was used as headquarters by Hitler's Foreign Minister Joachim von Ribbentrop. Since the late 1950s it has been a luxury hotel, with its own golf course, where Richard Nixon and Nikita Krushchev, among other notables, have been entertained.

Wolfgangsee

About 7km (4½ miles) further southeast from Fuschl lies the quaint little village of **St Gilgen**. Stretched along the northern shore of Wolfgangsee (Wolfgang Lake), it is a popular destination for holiday-makers in summer and winter. The Wolfgangsee itself is 10km (6 miles) long and 2km (1½ miles) wide. With water temperatures of around 26°C (78°F) in summer, it is popular for watersports of all kinds.

St Gilgen is famed as the birthplace of Mozart's mother, Anna Pertl (1720–78). Although the composer himself never came here, there is now a **Mozart memorial room** (open June–Sept Tue–Sun 10am–noon and 3–6pm; admission fee) in the house where his mother was born. His sister Nannerl also lived in this house after her marriage, but she moved to Salzburg in 1801 when her husband died. The Mozart fountain and the parish church (1376) are also worth a visit.

For walkers and skiers, the Zwölferhorn lift takes you to the top of the Zwölferhorn mountain at 1,522m (4,993ft). In summer, the summit is a starting point for many alpine walks, while in winter, beginners and families ski here.

The village is also a good place from which to take a boat across the lake to **St Wolfgang**. The boats – some of which date from the 1880s – run a regular service from May to October. The journey is a wonderful way to appreciate the beauty of the countryside. Alternatively, you can drive the 18km (11 miles) along the whole of the southern shore of

Picturesque facades in the village of St Gilgen

the lake and along most of the northern shore until you reach St Wolfgang.

This village is probably the most overtly touristy of all the locations on the Wolfgangsee, but when you see it hugging the shore and protected by the Schafberg towering 1,783m (5,850ft) above it, you will understand why. The village has a long history as a pilgrimage destination following its foundation in 976 by St Wolfgang, the bishop of Regensburg. According to legend, he built the village's first small church, which is allegedly a site of miracle cures. It is certainly one of the most beautiful churches in the region. Inside, it has a winged altar created by Michael Pacher in 1481 and three Baroque altars by Meinrad Guggenbichler from 1706.

The village is also famous for its White Horse Inn, a hotel with a wonderful lakeside terrace. It was the inspiration for Ralph Benatzky's operetta *Im Weissen Rössl am Wolfgangsee*,

Sailing on the Wolfgangsee

which was first performed in Berlin in 1930.

A trip up the **Schafberg** on the funicular railway (May–Oct) is not to be missed. On a clear day, you have the most breathtaking view of the Salzkammergut with its lakes and mountains spread below. The railway was built at the end of the 19th century and has been operational for over 100 years. For steam train enthusiasts, the old steam-fired train does occasional nostalgia trips. For timetable and fare information, see <www.schafbergbahn.at>.

Decorative window shutter in St Wolfgang

Mondsee

The nearby lake of **Mondsee** lies approximately 30km (19m) east of Salzburg and is easily reached on the A1 motorway. An alternative route is the Romantikstrasse from St Gilgen, taking you under the Schafberg and along the western shore of the Mondsee. The lake has a reputation for being the warmest in the Salzkammergut and it is popular for all kinds of watersports in the summer. There are few settlements around the lake; the main one shares its name with the lake. The market town of Mondsee is worth visiting to see its church, originally part of a large Benedictine monastery. It was founded in 748, although construction of the church began in 1470. Built in Gothic style, it has a 17th-century Baroque interior. This was where the wedding scene in *The Sound of Music* was filmed.

WHAT TO DO

Salzburg is a very agreeable city for sightseeing. Most of the major sights are within easy walking distance of the centre. You can stroll around the Old Town, wander into the cathedral and other churches, relax in the large spacious squares, play outdoor chess, take a *Fiaker* (horse-drawn carriage ride) around the city or climb up the hill to see the fortress.

A pleasant way to relax in high summer is to sit on the grassy riverbank and watch the fast-flowing waters of the Salzach flow by, as well as the hustle and bustle of city life. If you want to get on the water, you can take a boat trip on the *Amadeus Salzburg*, which docks near the Makartsteg (pedestrian bridge). This takes you up the river as far as Hellbrunn and back again (<www.salzburgschifffahrt.at>).

CULTURE AND NIGHTLIFE

It is impossible to ignore Mozart in Salzburg. There is his birthplace, the house that he grew up in, Mozartplatz with its statue of Mozart, Mozartsteg (bridge), the Mozart Festival, Mozartkugeln (mini chocolate balls filled with marzipan) and the Wolfgang Amadeus Mozart Airport. But young Wolfgang is far from the only cultural feature to this city. The museums and galleries offer everything from Stone Age relics and Roman

Mozart's 250th

In 2006, Salzburg played a major role in the 250th birthday celebrations of Mozart. The festivities included a rare staging of all 22 of Mozart's operas during the Salzburg Festival. These are now available to buy on DVD.

A performance of *Jedermann (Everyman)* at the Salzburg Festival

The Large Festival Hall

remains to vintage aeroplanes and modern art.

Music and the performing arts are everywhere. All year round, operas and concerts are performed in the Festival Halls. The Landestheater (state theatre) and smaller theatres host musicals, ballets, operas and drama.

Festivals

The internationally famous **Salzburg Festival** (Salzburger Festspiele) is held every year from the last week in July to the end of August. Throughout the day you can hear opera singers practising through open windows, and every evening the Festival Halls and squares play host to magnificent operas and orchestral concerts. During the five-week period more than 180 events take place, including operas, concerts, plays and ballets, attracting the highest calibre of artists. If you are visiting Salzburg at this time and have not booked well in advance, there is very little accommodation to be had.

Many other festivals take place in Salzburg throughout the year. Among them is **Mozartwoche**, held each January *(see page 52)*. The **Easter Festival**, every March or early April. sees the Berlin Philharmonic relocate to Salzburg for two weeks to perform various operatic and orchestral productions. The **Whitsun Festival**, a four-day festival of Baroque music, takes place in May over the Whitsun weekend.

Karneval (Carnival) is the ball season all over Austria, and in the Roman Catholic areas of Germany. The ball season begins properly with the New Year's Eve celebrations and continues right up to Shrove Tuesday *(Faschingsdienstag)*, the last day before Lent (normally in February), when it culminates in a big celebration in which everybody dresses up in fancy dress and goes out to party. New Year's Eve and *Fasching* are the only two days of the year when the bars and taverns do not have to close.

All through the summer many individual streets hold festivals as well, with stalls and street theatre. In late August or early September, the **harvest festivals** begin, running until Austria's National Day on 26 October. Numerous events take place in the city of Salzburg and all the towns and villages in the province. These include church thanksgiving services,

Winter Wonderland

From the beginning of December until 6 January (Epiphany), the city becomes a winter wonderland, taken over by Christmas market stalls, ice sculptures, food and *Glühwein* stands and carol singers. It is a great social occasion enjoyed by residents and tourists alike. The largest Christmas market is held on Residenzplatz and Domplatz, while Mozartplatz becomes an ice rink. There are other markets in Mirabell Platz, Sterngarten (near the Sternbräu restaurant just off Getreidegasse), the Fortress Courtyard (weekends only) and Hellbrunn Palace.

On 6 December, St Nikolaus Day, the saint delivers his bag of goodies (traditionally chocolate) to well-behaved children. However, on 5 December, the city is visited by the Krampus – a devil-like horned creature who rushes around punishing naughty children. In fact, there are usually several Krampuses at large; you will know they are near when you hear their bells or the screams of the children. Keep a safe distance: Krampuses have permission to hit people!

brass band music (with sausages and beer), craft and farmers' markets, carved pumpkin displays, petting farms and other activities for children, and the taking down of the maypole that has been standing since the beginning of May. You will recognise the places holding harvest festivals by the large hay statues creatively constructed from bales and other paraphernalia. Take the opportunity to sample the local products, such as *Sturm*, fermented grape juice. Stiegl (the local brewery) normally brings out an autumn beer too.

Nightlife

Salzburg's varied nightlife offers bars, pubs, wine bars and taverns to suit all ages, tastes and budgets. Taverns like Zum Fidelen Affen and Gasthaus Wilder Mann are a must for beer lovers who want to experience the Austrian brew at its finest. Food is normally served here as well. The main streets for

Enjoying home-brewed ale at the Augustiner Brewery

bars are Rudolfskai, Gstättengasse, Kaigasse and Giselakai. Clubs do not really exist in Salzburg city centre; instead particular bars, such as Republic and the Shamrock Irish Bar, have designated dance areas.

For fans of Mozart, the **Mozart Dinner Concert** in St Peter's Stiftskeller (tel: 828 695-0) is the perfect evening entertainment. Exquisite soloists and a small chamber orchestra perform pieces of *Don Giovanni*, *The Marriage of Figaro* and *The Magic Flute* between the three courses of a meal prepared according to traditional 18th-century recipes.

Between May and October, you might consider the 'Sound of Salzburg Dinner Show', an entertainment-and-dining package all in English. The show takes place at the Sternbräu Dinner Theater, Getreidegasse 34 (tel: 826 617), and begins with a video entitled *Maria von Trapp – the True Story*. The stage show includes melodies from *The Sound of Music*, a 'Trapp Family Folk Music Revival' and a tribute to Mozart, performed in period costumes.

SHOPPING

Salzburg has plenty of outlets for the dedicated shopper: modern shopping centres, specialist stores and antique shops, designer boutiques and high-street fashion, and several wonderful markets selling fresh produce, arts, crafts and souvenir trinkets. The shopping centres are just a short bus ride from the centre of town (Europark, route No. 1 or 6, and Alpenstrasse, No. 3, 5 or 8), but everything else is within walking distance.

The main shopping streets in the city centre are Getreidegasse, in the Old Town, and Linzergasse across the river in the New Town. Here you will find individual designer boutiques and chain stores alongside bakeries, jewellers and supermarkets. If you explore the many lanes that lead off Getreidegasse to Universitätsplatz, Judengasse, Kaigasse,

Shopping on Universitätsplatz

Papagenoplatz and Steingasse, you will come across shops that deal in antiques, art, sculptures, perfumes, handmade soap, shoes, music and gifts. You can even buy Christmas tree decorations and Easter eggs all year round.

There's a fresh produce market, called Grünmarkt, Monday to Saturday on Universitätsplatz, where vegetables, fruit, meat, poultry, fish, seafood, pastries, cheeses, flowers, crafts and spices create a feast of colours and smells. The Schrannenmarkt is similar, held every Thursday 5am–1pm in front of St Andrew's Church on Mirabellplatz. In both of these markets there are many snack stands selling traditional treats, which are worth trying. During the late spring and summer months, there is sometimes a market called Salzachgalerien held at the weekends on the Old Town side of the Salzach. This is where local artists and craftspeople come to display and sell their work. On the first Sunday of every month 9am–4pm, there is a big flea-market on the horse-racing track (direction Freilassing).

SPORTS

The city and the province of Salzburg offer a wide range of activities for all seasons. During the winter you have the option of downhill and cross-country skiing, snowboarding, ice-skating and tobogganing. While in summer you can choose from golf, hiking, horse-riding, summer tobogganing, mountain biking and climbing, paragliding, watersports and canyoning or white-water rafting. Check with the tourist information office, the receptionist in your hotel or in youth hostels for up-to-date information on companies offering activity excursions.

Winter Sports

Salzburg's professional ice hockey team, the Red Bulls, have their home arena in the Volksgarten (Eisarena). The hockey season starts in late August and continues until March. If you are in Salzburg and the team is playing, you should get tickets as early as possible from the Ice Arena (tel: 630 752). It is advisable to dress warmly.

From the first snowfall, children make the field behind the fortress their winter playground. Makeshift toboggans compete with high-tech versions in sliding down the hill. Anyone is free to join in, and there is no entrance fee.

Salzburg is a well-located city for skiing and snowboarding, with some of the best slopes in the world within relatively easy reach. The province has hosted the Alpine Skiing World Championships, as well as ski jumping and snowboarding competitions. Whether you are an absolute beginner or an experienced skier, you will find a slope to suit your needs. Most of the major ski resorts are to the south of Salzburg, the nearest being just 20 minutes away and the best of them between 45 and 90 minutes from the city. The resorts offer a wide choice of accommodation, including

An Alpine skiing centre

slope-side alpine cabins, as well as numerous shops, restaurants, banks and a good nightlife. Off-piste skiing, cross-country, ice-skating, tobogganing and night skiing are just some of the additional activities you can do. Among the ski areas within comfortable travelling distance of Salzburg are Flachau, Obertauern, Badgastein, Zell Am See and Saalbach-Hinterglemm.

The best way to get to the resorts from Salzburg is by train, leaving early in the morning. The information desk at the railway station will be able to advise you about the best way to get to your destination. If you are staying in Salzburg during the winter season and would like to go skiing for just one or two days, a Snow Shuttle bus leaves Mirabellplatz every morning to a different destination. One day you might be in Flachau, the next you could be in Kitzbühel, but every evening you can be back in Salzburg. (For more information on the Snow Shuttle, *see page 124*.)

Watersports

Salzburg offers a choice of many outdoor swimming pools, which are well maintained and very clean. All have lifeguards on duty, as well as snack bars and restaurants. Some even have diving pools and crazy golf. The outdoor pools *(freibad)* are at the following locations: Leopoldskron (bus No. 15), Volksgarten (bus No. 6 or 7) and Alpenstrasse (bus No. 3, 5 or 8). There is also an indoor swimming pool in the city centre at Paracelsus Bad und Kurhaus, Auerspergstrasse 2. If you would prefer to head out to the alpine lakes, with crystal-clear water and breathtaking views, the easiest thing to do is to catch a Post Bus from the railway station or from Mirabellplatz. All kinds of watersports are on offer at the lakes, including windsurfing, water skiing, sailing and fishing.

The Alpen Therme water park in Bad Hofgastein has everything from saunas and slides, to beautiful outdoor pools with a panoramic view of the Alps (open Sat–Wed 9am–9pm, Thur–Fri 9am–10pm).

Cycling

Salzburg is a very bike-friendly city. There are scenic cycle paths everywhere along the river, through Nonntal to Leopoldskron, Moosstrasse, Mülln and Anif (Hellbrunn). A few cycling tips: stick to the cycle paths, know your hand signals, and be aware of other cyclists who tend to overtake at great speed. In Salzburg, it is not a legal obligation to wear a helmet, though it is much safer to do so. At night you must use front and back lights. For pedestrians: do not walk on the cycle paths; when you hear a bell ringing, watch out, and move out of the way. If your hotel or hostel does not offer free bike loan, *see page 106* for bike hire details.

Cycling on the Grossglockner High Alpine Road

Hiking

Salzburg and its surrounding area offer all levels of hiking. A good city walk goes from Mülln, over the Mönchsberg, through town and finishes off on the Kapuzinerberg. For something out of town but not too demanding, try the Gaisberg (to the east) which has a road all the way to the top. You can walk parallel with it, which makes finding the way easy. The view from the top of Gaisberg is breathtaking. If you want to push yourself and get away from the city, the Untersberg is perfect. Really adventurous types will find plenty of trekking routes in the Salzkammergut. Make sure you have an idea of the weather and save your hikes for clear days. You should buy a hiking guide that details rest huts and routes along the trails.

SALZBURG FOR CHILDREN

The best attractions for children are Hellbrunn Palace with its novelty water fountains and zoo, the Open Air Museum in Grossgmain, Salzburg's Toy Museum with playthings from all over Europe, and the Natural History Museum. The latter is interactive, so even though the descriptions are in German, kids can still get involved. Ice-skating takes place all year round in the Volksgarten and during the Christmas season on Mozartplatz. Children are thrilled by the Krampus runs in the first week of December. Summer brings swimming (pools are supervised by lifeguards), cycling and street theatre. Outside the city, try the Alpen Therme water park in Bad Hofgastein.

Christmas magic at Hellbrunn

Calendar of Events

For the most up-to-date information and comprehensive listing of events, contact the tourist information office *(see page 126)*. Also, keep an eye on posters and billboards around the city.

January New Year's Eve festivities continue through the night, with fireworks, live music and waltzing on Residenzplatz. Ball season is in full swing. *Mozartwoche* (Mozart Week) at the end of January sees 10 days of performances of Mozart's music to mark the composer's birthday on 27 January.

February Carnival season ends with *Faschingsdienstag* (Shrove Tuesday) when fancy dress and partying take over the city.

March–April The Easter Festival is celebrated with opera productions and orchestral performances over two weeks.

May Baroque music is performed during the four-day *Salzburger Pfingstfestspiele* (Whitsun Festival).

June Midsummer festivals take place on the longest day of the year: beacons are lit on the highest peaks throughout Austria.

June–July The *SommerSzene* festival celebrates the art of modern dance, with dancers and choreographers from all over the world. Street theatre and markets.

July–August *Salzburger Festspiele*, the Salzburg Festival, begins during the last week in July and continues until the end of August, commemorating the music of Mozart and other great composers. Attracts large crowds. Street theatre and markets.

September Harvest festivals take place throughout Salzburg province, with church services, craft and farmers' markets.

October Salzburg Culture Days *(Kulturtage)* is a two-week festival of opera and classical music, second only to the *Salzburger Festspiele*.

October–November The last few days of October see the beginning of *Salzburger Jazz Herbst* (Salzburg Jazz Festival).

November The Christmas markets begin at the end of November.

December Christmas festivities take place throughout the city – markets, mulled wine, carol singers, ice-skating and ice sculptures.

EATING OUT

Salzburg has a strong tradition of dining out. The oldest eatery in the city bears witness to this: the Peter's Keller was established as a tavern by the monks of St Peter's in 803. Ever since, the people of Salzburg have enjoyed eating in restaurants and taverns. You will often see whole families gathered around a restaurant table, or large groups of friends out celebrating a special occasion. Meals are not hurried and it is not unusual for people to spend a whole evening in a restaurant relishing a hefty three-course meal, with beer and wine flowing freely.

WHAT TO EAT

It is very evident that Austrian cuisine is still more seasonal than in many other countries. Until the country joined the EU in 1995, the choice of products available in the shops was limited to those grown and produced in Austria, with imports mainly coming from Italy. Since then, however, the choice has widened immensely, although you will still not find the vast array of convenience foods found in some supermarkets in the Anglo-Saxon world.

Salzburg has collected influences from all over Europe, especially the Austro-Hungarian Empire and, more recently, has been inspired by international cuisine from around the globe. The Turks brought coffee and the coffee culture to Austria during

Local delicacies

Salzburg specialities include the ubiquitous *Salzburger Nockerl* (a very rich pudding made of fruit and soft meringue) and the local savoury delicacies *Kaspressknödel* (a bread dumpling flavoured with cheese) and *Fleischkrapfen* (large pockets of pasta with a meat filling).

the siege of Vienna in the 17th century; *Gulasch* and salamis come from the Hungarian part of the Austro-Hungarian Empire and some people even claim that the *Schnitzel* originated in Italy.

Meat

Traditionally, Austrian food has evolved around meat. Pork is the most popular item on the menu, closely followed by beef. Two of the classic meat dishes are *Schweinsbraten* (roast pork) and *Zwiebelrostbraten* (roast beef with gravy and onions). If you are a hungry carnivore and find it difficult to make up your mind, a *Grillteller* (mixed grill) is always a good choice for sharing.

Vegetables

Vegetables are beginning to play a more important role in Austrian cuisine and you will still find a lot of seasonal dishes. If you are here in the summer, the wild mushrooms are wonderful. In winter, the root vegetables come into their own; *Schwarzwurzel* (black salsify) and *Kohlrabi* (a member of the cabbage family) are among the most popular. Finding good vegetarian food in Austria used to be a hopeless cause, but now nearly all restaurants offer a vegetarian alternative. There are also several vegetarian

Lunch on the Mönchsberg rock

eateries *(see pages 135–42)*. Organic food is very popular here and you will find several restaurants and shops offering *Bio* produce.

Seasonal Specialities

No matter what time of year you visit Salzburg, there is always some seasonal speciality on offer. In spring and early summer it's asparagus; in late summer it's *Eierschwammerl* (chanterelle mushrooms); in autumn it's game; in November it's goose; and at Christmas it is mulled wine and roast chestnuts. Austrians do not have a typical Christmas meal. Here it is traditional to eat fish on Christmas Eve, but steak or any other special treat are also options. Gingerbread and Christmas biscuits are the sweet specialities. On New Year's Eve, a fondue with either cheese or meat is a typical dish as it makes for a genial atmosphere around the table.

Traditional Austrian fare – *Wienerschnitzel*

Bread and Cheese

If you are looking for a snack or a light lunch, the wonderful dark Austrian breads are perfect to enjoy with a plate of Austrian cheeses or *Speck* (a dry-smoked bacon). There are many different types of cheese, ranging from strong-flavoured hard mountain cheeses, to more gently flavoured soft cheese dips and spreads.

The patisserie at Café Sacher

Desserts

During the hardships of World War II, people had to make do with the ingredients available to them. This has led to a love of desserts made from eggs, flour and milk. Many of the sweet dumpling, cakes and pancake-type dishes stem from these times. Although made from the simplest of ingredients, they can all be extremely delicious.

Coffee and Cakes

The city is awash with cafés of all styles, and anybody spending a few days here will see that they play an important role in the social life of Salzburg's citizens. Nobody is in a hurry. The coffee-house culture here means that you can sit over one cup of coffee, reading the café's newspapers and magazines, for as long as you want. This is just as well, as the first glance at the menu will reveal that coffee is not simply coffee. There are many types to choose from. All coffee served is made with espresso machines (the only time you might be served filter coffee is with breakfast in your hotel). The following list

Delicious *Sachertorte*

should help in choosing the right coffee.

Verlängerter: A 'normal' cup of coffee made with one portion of espresso to two portions of water.

Espresso: One portion of espresso mixed with one of water.

Cappuccino: One part espresso to one of warm milk and one of whisked milk.

Latte/Macchiato: A double espresso in a large cup or glass topped with warm milk and foam.

Melange: One portion of coffee, two measures of water and warm milk.

Einspänner: One portion of black coffee served in a tall glass with whipped cream and icing sugar on top.

Fiaker: A single espresso served in a glass with a dash of rum.

You will also notice that you will be served a small glass of tap water with your coffee. This is a tradition that was brought in by the Turks. Their coffee was (and still is) famously 'sludgy', so it was normal to serve a glass of water with which to wash down the grounds. Nowadays this is no longer necessary, but the tradition has remained.

Of course, coffee is not the sole focus of these places – an amazing array of cakes and buns is on offer. Choosing a cake can be quite daunting when faced with so many different, delicious-looking cream cakes, fruit flans, biscuits and other sweet delights. The most famous are *Sachertorte* (a chocolate cake) and *Apfelstrudel* (apples and raisins wrapped in thin layers of pastry). But there are many others to tempt you. The *Cremeschnitte* is a cream slice; *Topfen* is cream curd used in many cakes that are often topped with seasonal fruits or berries; *Linzertorte* is a tart with jam and nuts. *Mandeln* (almonds) are also used in many biscuits and cakes; a particularly good one is *Bienenstich* (literally 'bee sting'), a cake base filled with whipped cream and almonds with honey on top. A wonderfully gooey biscuit is the *Florentiner* (nuts and candied fruit covered in chocolate).

WHAT TO DRINK

Salzburg is split between the beer and the wine lovers, and both are well catered for.

Beer

With three locally brewed beers on offer – Stiegl, Kaiser and Augustiner – all with long histories, you will almost certainly find a beer to your taste. You should try the *Weissbier* at least once. This is a cloudy beer as the yeast has not been entirely brewed out. It comes in a light and dark form, with the

Austrian Fast Food

It is hard to miss the usual fast-food outlets in Austria, but the international brand names are popular mainly with youngsters and tourists. True Austrian fast food comes in the form of the sausage stand. These are scattered all over the city and you can usually find at least one open at any time of night or day. Sausages are available in all shapes and sizes, including *Weisswurst* from Munich, *Frankfurters* (hot dogs), *Bosna* (served with mustard, ketchup and onions in a roll) and *Käsekrainer* (contains pieces of cheese).

dark version being somewhat sweet. *Zwickel* is another slightly cloudy brew. *Bockbier* is available at certain times of year, usually Christmas and Easter, and is a stronger special brew which should be handled with care – perhaps start with just a *Pfiff* (200 millilitres) to test the effect. The beer-garden culture is alive in the summer, and sitting in one of the leafy gardens, enjoying a beer or two, is a wonderful way to spend an evening.

Salzburg's taverns or *Gasthäuser* are an excellent combination of beer-hall and restaurant. You will often find some of the best Austrian food served in these establishments at very reasonable prices. For the most part they are traditional old taverns that have retained their wooden interiors and are cool in summer and cosy in winter.

A classic beer snack

Wine

If you have never tried Austrian wines, then the wine bars and restaurants in Salzburg are a good place to start. Although this is not a wine-growing region, wines from Styria, Burgenland and Lower Austria are all worth trying. After the Austrian wine scandal in the 1980s, many winegrowers had to lift their game, and now produce extremely high-quality wines in order to prove that most of the Austrian vineyards should be taken seriously. Both the red and white wines are very palatable and the most common are: *Grüner Veltliner*, a light, dry, crisp white wine; *Welschriesling*, a fresh, fruity white wine; *Zweigelt*, a full-bodied dry red; and *Blauer Burgunder* (Pinot Noir), a fruity, soft red. If you do not know what to choose, your waiter will be happy to recommend a good bottle for you.

Steins of beer at the Augustiner Brewery

When in Austria in the late summer and early autumn, you should try *Sturm*. This is grape juice that is still fermenting and is very refreshing. The white variety tends to be drier than the red one.

Another Austrian speciality is *Schnaps*. This is a strong, clear spirit produced using a variety of different fruits. The most commonly available types are *Obstler*, made from apples and pears, *Marillenschnaps*, made from apricots, and *Vogelbeer*, made from rowanberries. Try one after dinner as a digestif. They are also commonly used as cure-alls in Austrian households.

To Help You Order…

Do you have a table for two/four?	**Haben Sie einen Tisch für zwei/vier Personen, bitte?**
Could we have the menu?	**Die Speisekarte, bitte?**
I/we would like…	**Ich hätte/Wir hätten gern…**
Could we have the bill please?	**Zahlen, bitte.**

...And Read the Menu

Auflauf	soufflé or a dish baked with cheese on top
Backhendl	chicken sautéed in egg and breadcrumbs
Bauernschmaus	meat with dumplings and sauerkraut
Blaukraut	red cabbage
Blunzn	black pudding
Bosna	spicy sausages in a roll with onions, curry powder, mustard and ketchup
Brot	bread
Buchteln/Wuchteln	yeast buns filled with jam
Debreziner	spicy Hungarian sausage
Eierschwammerl	chanterelle mushrooms
Fleischlaberl	meat rissoles
Frittatensuppe	clear soup with sliced pancakes
Gefüllte Paprika	stuffed peppers
Germknödel	big, fluffy yeast dumplings
Griessnockerlsuppe	semolina dumpling soup
Gugelhupf	Viennese sponge cake
Kaiserschmarrn	pancake served with raisins and apple sauce
Kartoffelsalat	potato salad
Kasspatzln	pasta with cheese and fried onions
Knödel	flour, potato or yeast dumpling
Krautsalat	shredded white cabbage salad with caraway seeds
Marillenknödel	apricot dumpling
Palatschinken	pancakes with various fillings

Ribisel	red or blackcurrants
Rostbraten	pot roast
Salzburger Nockerl	dessert with sponge cake, fruit and soft meringue
Schinkenfleckerl	baked noodles with ham
Schwammerlsuppe	mushroom soup
Schweinsbraten	roast pork
Semmel	bread roll
Senf	mustard
Tafelspitz	boiled beef
Topfenknödel	dumpling made with curd
Wienerschnitzel	veal or pork escalope fried in breadcrumbs
Zigeunerschnitzel	pork escalope in paprika sauce
Zwiebelrostbraten	beef steak with fried onions

Salzburger Nockerl

HANDY TRAVEL TIPS

An A–Z Summary of Practical Information

A Accommodation . . 105
Airport 105
B Bicycle Hire 106
Budgeting for
Your Trip 106
C Camping 107
Car Hire 108
Chemists 108
Climate 109
Clothing 109
Complaints 109
Crime and Safety . 110
Customs and Entry
Requirements . . . 110
D Driving 111
E Electricity 114
Embassies and
Consulates 114
Emergencies 114
G Gay and Lesbian
Travellers 115
Getting There 115
Guides and Tours . 116
H Health and
Medical Care . . . 117

L Language 117
Laundry 118
Lost Property 118
M Maps 118
Media 119
Money Matters . . . 119
O Opening Hours . . . 120
P Police 121
Post Offices 121
Public Holidays . . . 122
Public Transport . . 122
R Religion 123
S Snow Shuttle 124
T Taxis 124
Telephone 124
Tickets 124
Time Zones 125
Tipping 125
Toilets 125
Tourist
Information 126
Travellers with
Disabilities 126
W Websites 127
Y Youth Hostels 127

A

ACCOMMODATION (see also CAMPING, YOUTH HOSTELS and RECOMMENDED HOTELS on page 128)

Salzburg has a wide selection of accommodation including the usual chain hotels such as Radisson, Sheraton, Mercure and Dorint, but also offers privately run hotels that tend to be friendlier and more characterful.

For most of the year it is not necessary to book accommodation in advance, but during peak times (July, August, December and Easter) advance reservations are essential. The Salzburg Tourist Office website, <www.salzburg.info.at>, offers an online booking service, in English as well as German. They also publish a booklet of accommodation every year, though this is not a complete listing of all the hotels and guesthouses in the city.

If you have not booked somewhere to stay before you arrive, the tourist information offices at the railway station and on Mozartplatz can assist with finding accommodation.

Pensionen are the equivalent of guesthouses or bed and breakfasts, and are less expensive than hotels.

a guesthouse	**eine Pension**
a single/double room	**ein Einzelzimmer/Doppelzimmer**
with/without bath (shower)	**mit/ohne Bad (Dusche)**
What's the rate per night?	**Was kostet eine Übernachtung?**

AIRPORT (Flughafen)

Salzburg's airport, W. A. Mozart, <www.salzburg-airport.com>, is located on the western edge of the city. The airport is small, but offers all the usual facilities: restaurant, bar, banks, shops, cafés and a newsagent. There are regular public transport connections by bus to the railway station (direct) and the city centre (change of bus).

The journey to the station takes approximately 30 minutes. There is also a taxi rank directly outside the arrivals terminal. All car-hire offices are across the road in the multi-storey car park.

Arrivals are always through Terminal I, but in winter all the ski charter flights depart from the new Terminal II.

B

BICYCLE HIRE (Fahrradverleih)

Salzburg has a superb network of cycle paths around the city and along the riverbanks, and it's possible to travel quite some distance without having to tackle any real hills. Many hotels, pensions and youth hostels offer free bike loan. If yours does not, there are plenty of bike-hire shops in the city. **Top Bike Salzburg** (tel: 0676-476 7259 and 062-724 656) is situated close to the Staatsbrücke. They have bikes and also rent out audio guides to the sights in English.

A new cycle path, named after Wolfgang Amadeus Mozart, now runs from the city through the Salzburg Lake District (Salzkammergut) and on to Bavaria and its lakes, before ending at Berchtesgaden, near Hitler's former holiday retreat *(see page 67)*. The route stretches more than 410km (250 miles) and is primarily flat, with just a few hills along the way. It's ideal for families. Salzburg tourist offices will provide trail maps *(see page 126)*.

BUDGETING FOR YOUR TRIP

The currency in Austria is the euro. To give you a rough guide of how much things cost, the following is a list of average prices:

Airport: bus to railway station or city centre €1.80 for a single ticket.

Bicycle hire: €6 for 2 hours, €10 for 4 hours, €15 for a day.

Car hire: from around €70 for an economy class car for one day, €135 for a weekend.

Entertainment: cinema ticket around €8, entrance into a nightclub or disco from around €5.

Guides: a private city guide will cost about €150 for 3 hours.

Hotels: a double room with breakfast will cost €150 and upwards per night in a five-star hotel, between €40 and €65 in a one-star.

Meals: an average meal in Salzburg will cost between €15 and €30 per head including a drink.

Museums: admission fees vary greatly from one museum to the next; there are reductions for children and students. A Salzburg Card *(see page 9)* provides free admission to many museums.

Public transport: a single ticket costs €1.80 if you buy your ticket on the bus or from one of the machines, €1.60 if you buy it in advance. A day pass costs €3.40 in advance and €4.20 if bought from the driver.

Sightseeing: a *Fiaker* (horse-drawn carriage) trip for up to four people costs €36 for 20 minutes and €72 for a 50-minute tour. A boat trip on the *Amadeus Salzburg* costs €13–16 for adults and €8–10 for children. If you join a Salzburg city guide for a guided group tour, it costs €10 per person.

Taxis: in Salzburg taxis run on a meter; fares start at €3.50 during the day and €3.80 in the evening.

Tickets: concerts €10–60; Salzburger Landestheater €9–32 for a play and €16–50 for an opera; Marionette Theatre €20–35 for adults, €14 for children. Salzburg Festival: tickets here vary greatly in price according to the performance. See <www.salzburgfestival.at> for details.

C

CAMPING

There are four campsites in the vicinity of Salzburg: Nord Sam (tel: 660 494) and Camping Kasern (tel: 450 576), both open end Apr–early Oct, Camping Panorama Stadtblick (tel: 450 652, open end Mar–early Nov) and Camping Schloss Aigen (tel: 622 079, open May–Sept).

CAR HIRE (*Autovermietung*; see also DRIVING)

Driving in Salzburg is not recommended. It is easy to lose your bearings in the maze of one-way streets, and parking is either expensive or very difficult to find. However, should you require car hire for some trips out of town, most of the major car-hire companies have offices at the airport.

When hiring a car, make sure you have your driving licence, passport and one of the major credit cards with you. You will have to take out third-party insurance. Whether you take out fully comprehensive insurance is up to you. Do be aware that the excess is quite high if you damage the car.

Avis tel: 877 278, <www.avis.co.uk>
Budget tel: 855 038, <www.budget.co.uk>
Denzeldrive tel: 852 949, <www.denzel.at>
Europcar tel: 850 208, <www.europcar.co.uk>
Hertz tel: 852 086, <www.hertz.co.uk>

I'd like to rent a car tomorrow for one day/week Please include full insurance.	**Ich möchte bitte ein Auto mieten für morgen für einen Tag/für eine Woche Mit Vollkaskoversicherung, bitte.**

CHEMISTS (*Apotheke*)

In order to buy any sort of medication in Austria, you will have to go to a chemist. Should you require a chemist outside normal opening times, there is usually a duty roster posted on the door of all chemists.

Where is there a chemist on duty?	**Wo ist die diensthabende Apotheke?**

CLIMATE

Salzburg has a well-deserved reputation for being a rainy city and the watery weather even has a nickname: *Schnürlregen* (string-rain). It can rain for three seasons of the year, and in winter it snows instead. Salzburg can be exceedingly cold in winter and stiflingly hot in summer. The best times of year for visiting the city in pleasant temperatures are spring and autumn. In spring the alpine flowers are in full bloom, and in autumn the colours of the forest are aglow. At these times the streets are not filled to bursting point with tourists. If you are looking for some romantic winter atmosphere, then December, when the Christmas Market is in full swing, is also a good time, but much busier.

Below is a chart showing Salzburg's average temperatures and rainfall for the year:

	J	F	M	A	M	J	J	A	S	O	N	D
°C	1	4	11	16	20	24	25	24	21	15	8	2
°F	34	39	52	61	68	75	77	75	70	59	46	36
mm	54	49	41	52	73	110	134	108	81	67	53	46

CLOTHING

Whatever the time of year, it is always best to bring layers and something waterproof. It may be freezing cold outside in winter, but the buildings are all very well heated and insulated inside. There can be cold snaps in summer, so light jumpers or jackets can be useful.

Austrians dress casually for most occasions. They do like to be smart when going to the theatre, opera or ballet or a ball. Evening dress is often worn to festival performances.

COMPLAINTS

Should there be a problem with your accommodation, it is best to complain to the management. The same applies for restaurants or bars. If this does not bring about the desired effect, then you could complain at the tourist office. For serious complaints, speak to the police or go to your local consulate.

CRIME AND SAFETY

Salzburg is a very safe city. You do need to watch out for pickpockets in busy places (such as markets) and make sure you lock up your bicycle if you leave it anywhere. If you leave valuables in your car, ensure that they are out of sight and the car is locked.

CUSTOMS *(Zoll)* AND ENTRY REQUIREMENTS

A valid passport is required to enter Austria. If you are coming from an EU country, the US, Canada, Australia or New Zealand, you do not require a visa. See <www.bmeia.gv.at/london> for further information from the Austrian Embassy in London.

All goods brought into Austria from EU countries must be duty-paid. Visitors from non-EU countries can bring in the following duty-free items: 200 cigarettes or 50 cigars or 250g of tobacco; 2 litres of alcohol (of less than 22 percent), and 1 litre of alcohol (of over 22 percent).

Austria is a member of Schengen, the 24 EU countries that have signed a treaty to end internal border checkpoints and controls. This means that if you are arriving from another Schengen state (e.g. Germany, Italy) there are no more border controls. Police do, however, carry out spot checks on some routes near the borders.

I've nothing to declare.	**Ich habe nichts zu verzollen.**
It's for my personal use.	**Das ist für meinen persönlichen Gebrauch.**

Currency restrictions. There are no restrictions on the amount of foreign currency that can be brought into Austria.

VAT reimbursement. Non-EU citizens are entitled to reclaim VAT paid on goods over a certain value *(Mehrwehrtsteuer)*. On purchase you must obtain a U34 form from the shop assistant. If you get this stamped either at the airport or at the border when leaving the country, then send the form back to the shop and they will transfer the amount to your bank account.

D

DRIVING (See also CAR HIRE)

If you are taking your car to Austria, you must arrive with a valid driving licence, car registration papers, a national identity sticker for your car, a red warning triangle and a reflective high-visibility waistcoat in case of breakdown, and a first-aid kit (in winter you must also have snow chains if you are heading for the mountains).

To drive on Austrian motorways, you will require a toll sticker, called a *Vignette*. These are available for durations of between 10 days and a year. They are available from petrol stations, post offices and tobacconists.

driving licence	**Führerschein**
car registration papers	**Zulassungsschein**
Green Card	**Grüne Karte**
Where's the nearest car park, please?	**Wo ist der nächste Parkplatz, bitte?**
Can I park here?	**Darf ich hier parken?**
Are we on the right road for…?	**Sind wir auf der richtigen Strasse nach...?**
Check the oil/tires/battery, please.	**Öl/Reifen/Batterie prüfen, bitte.**
I've had a breakdown.	**Ich habe eine Panne.**
There's been an accident.	**Es ist ein Unfall passiert.**

Road conditions. The roads in Austria are very good on the whole. The north–south routes can get very busy at weekends in the summer, with many people driving to and from Croatia and Italy, and in winter, when people are heading to and from the ski resorts. Information on road conditions and the traffic situation is available in English seven days a week 6am–8pm (tel: 0043-1 711 997).

Driving regulations. Austrians drive on the right. Here are some of the rules of the road that you might find useful:
- It is compulsory to wear seatbelts in front and rear seats.
- It is forbidden to use a hand-held mobile phone while driving.
- Children under the age of 12 are not permitted to sit in the front.
- It is forbidden to overtake on the right on the motorway.
- Headlights must be switched on at all times.
- The alcohol limit is 0.5 parts per thousand.

Speed limits. On motorways 130km/h (81mph) or 110km/h (68mph); on other roads 100km/h or 80km/h (50mph); in built-up areas 50km/h (31mph).

Parking can be difficult in Salzburg. It is not permitted to park in the bus lanes during the stated times. If you do so, you will be towed away. If you park in a blue parking bay, you will need to pay and display a ticket (machines are located nearby).

Breakdowns. There is a 24-hour breakdown service for all drivers on the motorways and main roads. The two Austrian motoring clubs are ÖAMTC (tel: 120, <www.oeamtc.at>) and ARBÖ (tel: 123, <www.arboe.at>).

Fuel and oil. There are plenty of petrol stations around Salzburg. Not all are open 24 hours, but those on the motorway and at the major entrances to the city are. Petrol, diesel and LPG are available.

Leaded petrol cannot be bought in Austria. Certain pumps dispensing unleaded petrol contain a lead additive, for vehicles requiring leaded petrol.

Road signs. Most road signs employed in Austria are international, but here are some written signs you might come across:

Anfang	(parking) start
Ausfahrt	exit
Aussicht	viewpoint
Bauarbeiten	road works
Einbahnstrasse	one way
Ende	(parking) end
Fahrbahnwechsel	change lanes
Fußgänger	pedestrians
Gefahr	danger
Geradeaus	straight on
Glatteis	icy roads
Halten verboten	no stopping
Licht einschalten	use headlights
Ortsende	town ends
Parken erlaubt	parking allowed
Rechts/links einbiegen	turn right/left
Rollsplitt	loose gravel
Sackgasse	no through road
Spital	hospital
Steinschlag	falling stones
Umleitung	detour
Vorfahrt	priority
Vorsicht	caution
Werktags von 7 bis 17 Uhr	weekdays 7am to 5pm
Zufahrt gestattet	entrance permitted

E

ELECTRICITY

Austrian plugs have two round pins, so an adapter is necessary if your device has a British or US plug. The voltage here is 220 volts.

EMBASSIES AND CONSULATES *(Botschaft; Konsulat)*

Contact your consulate or embassy only for real emergencies, such as loss of a passport or all your money, a serious accident or trouble with the police. Citizens of most countries will have to contact their embassies in Vienna or a consulate in Munich. The consulate in Salzburg is:

UK: Alter Markt 4, 5020 Salzburg, tel: 848 133.

EMERGENCIES (See also CRIME AND SAFETY and POLICE)

Normally, in the case of an emergency, your hotel receptionist will be happy to assist. If you do need to get hold of the emergency services yourself, the numbers are as follows:

Police (emergency): **133**
Fire brigade: **122**
Ambulance, first aid: **144**
Emergency medical service: **141**
Emergency dentist: **870 022**

I need a doctor/ dentist/ambulance.	**Ich brauche einen Arzt/ Zahnarzt/Krankenwagen.**
Fire!	**Feuer!**
Help!	**Hilfe!**
hospital	**Spital**
police	**Polizei**

G

GAY AND LESBIAN TRAVELLERS

The gay and lesbian scene in Salzburg is not very evident. There are a few bars in the city that cater for gays and lesbians, including Zweistein on Giselakai and Diva in the Priesterhausgasse.

GETTING THERE

Travel information is constantly changing, so do check on the internet or with a travel agent to ensure you have entirely up-to-date information.

By Air

Scheduled flights. There are regular flights year-round from several UK airports, and from Dublin, to Salzburg. Ryanair, <www.ryanair.com>, has daily flights to Salzburg from London Stansted, and Thomsonfly, <www.thomsonfly.com>, offers flights from London Gatwick, Doncaster/Sheffield, Manchester, Coventry and Bournemouth.

Charter flights. During the summer and winter seasons there are charter flights from many UK and Republic of Ireland airports. These are normally sold on a seat-only basis unless you are booking a package. Many UK tour operators offer Salzburg as a city break. Check with your travel agent for details.

Via Munich. The choice of scheduled flights to Munich is much greater than to Salzburg. Munich is about 1½–2 hours away from Salzburg by train and 1½ hours by car.

By Car

Salzburg is a long drive from the UK and it is recommended that you take two days to reach it. Although the German motorways are pretty good, they can get very busy over the summer months. The quickest route is via Ostende, Cologne, Stuttgart and Munich.

The Austrian trains have car trains from Vienna and Feldkirch, where you can drive onto the train, or you can hop on in Munich. Contact Austrian Federal Railways (ÖBB) for details (tel: 05 1717, <www.oebb.at>) or the Deutsche Bahn (<www.bahn.de>).

By Coach

Contact Eurolines (tel: 08717-818181, <www.eurolines.co.uk>) for details of coach services from the UK to Salzburg.

By Rail

There are regular train services from London St Pancras International to Salzburg via Paris and Munich. The journey takes about 16 hours. Sleepers and couchettes are available if booked in advance. Contact ÖBB (tel: 05 1717, <www.oebb.at>) for further information.

GUIDES AND TOURS *(Fremdenführer, Rundfahrten)*

There are two major bus tour companies in Salzburg that offer guided tours of the city, both by coach and on foot, and also to places of interest nearby: Salzburg Sightseeing Tours (tel: 881 616, <www.salzburg-sightseeingtours.at>) and Panorama Tours (tel: 883 2110, <www.panoramatours.com>). Both have *The Sound of Music* tours, which visit all the film locations in and around the city. All these tours are in English.

The local tourist office also organises guided tours on foot with English-speaking guides; check in the tourist office at Mozartplatz.

Outside the Residenz you will find a row of horse-drawn carriages awaiting customers. These are known as *Fiakers* and will take you through the old town at a leisurely pace *(see page 107)*.

Boat trips on the Salzbach aboard the *Amadeus Salzburg* are available between May and September. They leave at regular intervals from the Makartsteg (pedestrian bridge) in the Old Town and take you as far as Hellbrunn Castle and the zoo.

We'd like an English-speaking guide.	**Wir möchten einen englisch-sprachigen Fremdenführer.**
I need an English interpreter.	**Ich brauche einen Dolmetscher für Englisch.**
How long will the ride take?	**Wie lange dauert die Fahrt?**
What does it cost?	**Was kostet es?**

H

HEALTH AND MEDICAL CARE (*Ärztliche Hilfe;* see also CHEMISTS)

The health service in Salzburg is excellent. There are numerous medical facilities, including an *Unfallkrankenhaus* (Accident Hospital) on Dr-Franz-Rehrl-Platz 5 (tel: 65 800) and Krankenhaus und Konvent der Barmherzigen Brüder, Kajetanerplatz 1 (tel: 80 880). The *Unfallkrankenhaus* is renowned for treating injured Austrian skiers. Austria and the UK have a reciprocal agreement as far as hospital treatment is concerned. EU citizens should arrive armed with a European Health Insurance Card (EHIC), available from post offices and online at <www.ehic.org.uk>, which entitles them to reduced-cost, sometimes free, medical treatment.

If you are taking prescription drugs, bring with you enough supply for the duration of your trip. The same drugs may not be available in Salzburg.

L

LANGUAGE

German is spoken in Austria. As Salzburg relies heavily on tourism, many of the people here speak at least a little English. But it is impolite to assume that everybody does, so you can try with a little German: *Entschuldigen Sie bitte* (Excuse me, please) is always appreciated. You could also ask, *Sprechen Sie Englisch?* (Do you speak English?), another good way to start. *The Berlitz German Phrase Book & Dictionary* covers most situations you may come across in Austria.

LAUNDRY AND DRY CLEANING

Getting clothes laundered or dry cleaned in Salzburg is expensive whichever way you do it. Most hotels offer a laundry service. There are many *Reinigung* (dry cleaners) around the city. Ask at your hotel reception to find out where the nearest one is. There is a reasonably priced coin-operated launderette opposite the railway station.

When will it be ready?	**Wann ist es fertig?**
For tomorrow morning, please.	**Bis morgen früh, bitte.**

LOST PROPERTY

The city lost property office is on the ground floor of the Mirabell Palace and is open Mon–Thur 7.30am–4pm, Fri 7.30am–1pm, tel: 8072 3580.

I've lost my passport/ wallet/handbag.	**Ich habe meinen Pass/ meine Brieftasche/ Handtasche verloren.**

MAPS

The tourist office gives away free street maps of Salzburg. They are relatively basic and it is a good idea to buy a more detailed one. Detailed city maps are available from the tourist office or from bookshops.

Maps of the bus routes can be picked up free in either the tourist information offices or from the railway station.

MEDIA

English-language newspapers are available at the airport, the railway station and some newsagents throughout the town. Most hotels also have a stock of the dailies. The English-language daily papers available in Salzburg are usually one day late.

Most of the hotels in Salzburg have cable TV. The programmes on offer vary, depending on the cable operator, but you should be able to get CNN and BBC World in English at least. If your hotel has satellite TV, you will probably have a greater choice of English-speaking channels.

On FM4, one of the ORF radio stations (104.6FM in Salzburg), you will find programmes are in English in the mornings. News reports are in English and French all day.

MONEY MATTERS *(Geld)*

Currency. Austria's monetary unit is the euro, symbolised €. The euro is divided into 100 cents. Banknotes in denominations of 500, 100, 50, 20, 10 and 5 are in circulation. There are coins to the value of 1 and 2 euros, 50, 20, 5, 2 and 1 cents.

Changing money. You can exchange your money at any of the banks in the city. Hotels and travel agents also offer money-exchange facilities, but their rates are not as good as those of the banks. All banks have ATM machines (cashpoints) and most of them accept UK debit cards. This is usually the most convenient way to obtain cash. Bureaux de change are also scattered throughout the city. These have the advantage of being open after the banks have closed. Travellers' cheques are widely accepted, but they do not give you as good an exchange rate as you would get in the banks.

Credit cards. The major credit cards are becoming more widely accepted in Austria. But some shops, bars and restaurants still do not accept them.

I want to change some pounds/dollars.	**Ich möchte Pfund/Dollar wechseln.**
Do you accept travellers cheques?	**Nehmen Sie Reiseschecks an?**
Do you have any change, please?	**Haben Sie Kleingeld, bitte?**
Where's the nearest cashpoint, please?	**Wo ist der nächste Geldautomat, bitte?**

OPENING HOURS

Shops. These can be divided into two categories when it comes to opening times. The first are the small shops in the shopping districts in town. These are mostly open from 9am until 6pm (some close for an hour or two at lunchtime) Mondays to Fridays and until 5pm on Saturdays. Supermarkets and shopping centres tend to be open from 9am until 7.30 or 8pm Mondays to Fridays and until 5pm on Saturdays. The only shops open on Sundays are those selling souvenirs.

Museums. These vary widely; for opening times check the individual entries in the Where to Go section.

Banks. Mon–Fri 8am–12.30pm and 2–4.30pm, Thur until 5.30pm.

Post offices. Mon–Fri 8am–noon and 2pm–5pm. The post office in the station is open Mon–Fri 7am–8.30pm, Sat 8am–2pm.

Chemists. Mon–Fri 8am–noon and 2pm–6pm, Sat 8am–noon.

P

POLICE (*Polizei*; see also CRIME AND SAFETY and EMERGENCIES)

Police have blue uniforms with dark blue baseball caps and carry guns. If you are fined for a traffic offence, you are likely to be asked to pay on the spot.

Street parking in Salzburg is supervised by traffic wardens, who wear dark blue trousers and white shirts.

In an emergency, contact the police on **133**.

Where is the nearest police station, please?	**Wo ist die nächste Polizeiwachstube, bitte?**

POST OFFICES (*Postamt*; see also OPENING TIMES)

Salzburg's main post office is at Residenzplatz 9. Ask your hotel receptionist for the location of the nearest one. If you just need stamps, you can also buy these from any tobacconist. Apart from letters and postcards, you can send packages, money orders and registered mail from post offices. Stamps and pre-paid telephone cards are sold there in various denominations, and most post offices also have pay and card phones from which you can make calls. Information on Austrian postal services can be found at: <www.post.at>. Salzburg's post boxes are yellow.

Express (special delivery)	**Express/Eilbote**
Airmail	**Luftpost**
Have you any mail for...?	**Haben Sie Post für...?**
A stamp for this letter/ postcard, please	**Eine Marke für diesen Brief/ diese Postkarte, bitte.**
I want to fax a letter to...	**Ich möchte einen Brief nach...faxen.**

PUBLIC HOLIDAYS (Feiertag)

There are a number of public holidays in Austria. On these days all offices and banks, most shops and some restaurants are closed. Note that on Good Friday, a holiday for Protestants only, shops etc remain open. On 24 December (Christmas Eve) all theatres and cinemas are closed, and most shops and restaurants close at midday.

1 January	*Neujahrstag*	New Year's Day
6 January	*Heilige Drei Könige*	Epiphany
1 May	*Tag der Arbeit*	Labour Day
15 August	*Maria Himmelfahrt*	Assumption
26 October	*Nationalfeiertag*	National Holiday
1 November	*Allerheiligen*	All Saints' Day
8 December	*Maria Empfängnis*	Immaculate Conception
25 December	*Weihnachten*	Christmas Day
26 December	*Stefanitag*	Boxing Day
Movable dates:	*Ostermontag*	Easter Monday
	Christi Himmelfahrt	Ascension Day
	Pfingstmontag	Whit Monday
	Fronleichnam	Corpus Christi

Are you open tomorrow? **Haben Sie morgen geöffnet?**

PUBLIC TRANSPORT

Buses. Salzburg has a very efficient public transport system. You will find maps of the bus and trolley bus routes at the railway station and the bus information office on Mirabellplatz. It is possible to buy tickets from the driver on getting on the bus and from the machines at some of the main bus stops, but it's cheaper to buy your tickets in advance. They are available from tobacconists (all marked with the

Austria Tabak sign). You can buy blocks of five single tickets, 24-hour tickets or weekly tickets. Consider buying a Salzburg Card *(see page 9)*, which includes free bus travel for the card's duration.

Post buses. These serve the outlying districts. Timetables can again be found at the railway station. You need to pay the driver when getting on the bus. Tickets cannot be bought in advance.

Lokalbahn. This commuter-train route serves many destinations to the north of the city, including Oberndorf and Maria Plain. Information is available at the railway station.

What's the fare to... ?	**Wieviel kostet es nach...?**
Where is the nearest bus stop?	**Wo ist die nächste Bushaltestelle?**
When's the next bus to...?	**Wann geht der nächste Bus nach...?**
I want a ticket to... single/return	**Ich will eine Fahrkarte nach... einfache Karte/Rückfahrkarte**
Will you tell me when to get off?	**Könnten Sie mir bitte sagen, wann ich aussteigen muss?**

R

RELIGION

Most Austrians are Roman Catholics, but there are Protestant minorities scattered throughout the country and also many Muslim communities. English-language Catholic services are held every Sunday at the Sacellum on Herbert-von-Karajan-Platz at 5pm. Anglican services in English are held in the Christus Kirche on Schwarzstrasse every Sunday at 11am.

The synagogue is at Lasserstrasse 8.

S

SNOW SHUTTLE

During the ski season, the tourist board organises a daily bus service to various ski resorts in the vicinity. The bus leaves from Mirabellplatz every morning and returns in the evenings. For more information, call the Snow Shuttle information line on 871 712.

T

TAXIS

Taxi stands are scattered throughout the city and can be found at the railway station or at the airport. If you need to order a taxi, ask at your hotel reception or call 8111 for the taxi switchboard.

TELEPHONE

Try to avoid using the phone in your hotel room: hotels can charge well over the odds for any calls you might make. Your best bet is to buy an international calling card (available from tobacconists or internet cafés) and use this for making calls. There are also public phones in all post offices, with instructions in English.

The international dialling code for Austria is 43 and the code for Salzburg is 0662 (leave off the first 0 if calling from overseas). To make an international call from Austria, dial 00 and then the country code (44 for the UK, 1 for the USA and Canada) and again omit the first zero from your area code.

TICKETS

Salzburg Festival. Tickets for the Salzburg Festival go on sale in November and can be booked online at <www.salzburgfestival.at>. The festival ticket office in Salzburg is situated at Herbert-von-Karajan-Platz 1 (tel: 8045 500). There are also a number of ticket agencies in the city, but they do charge quite a hefty booking fee.

You can try Polzer Ticket Service on Residenzplatz (tel: 846 500, <www.polzer.at>). They have tickets for all events in the area from rock concerts to operas.

Mozart Festival. Tickets for the Mozart Festival in January can be booked with the Mozarteum (tel: 889 400, <www.mozarteum.at>).

Other events. Tickets for the Marionette Theatre can be booked directly with their box office (tel: 872 406). The Mozart Dinner Concert can be booked online (<www.salzburg-concerts.com>) or at the box office before the start of a performance (tel: 828 695-0).

TIME ZONES

The time in Austria is Central European Time, which is one hour ahead of GMT. There is summer and winter time with the clocks going forward one hour at the end of March and back one hour at the end of October. The time differences are as follows:

New York	London	**Salzburg**	Jo'burg	Sydney	Auckland
6am	11am	**noon**	noon	8pm	10pm

TIPPING

In bars, restaurants and cafés it is customary to tip around 10 percent, even when a service charge is included in some restaurants. For smaller amounts, it is normal to round up. Although service charges are included in hotel bills, porters and chambermaids do expect a tip. Tour guides, taxi drivers and hairdressers also rely heavily on the tips they receive.

TOILETS

There are many public toilets around the city. They are found at the railway station, between Domplatz and Kapitelplatz, in the Altstadt

Garage Nord, on Hanuschplatz, Universitätsplatz, Mirabellplatz and Gardens and by the river on the Linzergasse side of the Staatsbrücke. There is usually a 50-cent charge for any toilet with an attendant.

You can use the facilities in any bar or restaurant without ordering, but it is not greatly appreciated. *Damen* means 'Ladies' and *Herren* means 'Gents'.

TOURIST INFORMATION

The **Salzburg Tourism Office** has a website in English: <www.salzburginfo.at>. This includes a list of accommodation, plus all the sights to see, places to visit and events on offer in Salzburg. You can book accommodation online.

In Salzburg, the tourist information offices are at the railway station and on Mozartplatz. You can get help in finding accommodation, obtain maps, book day trips and guided tours, and buy tickets.

The website of the Austrian National Tourist Office (ANTO, <www.austria.info>) is worth looking at because it also has a wealth of information about Salzburg. Their offices overseas can be found at the following addresses:

Australia: ANTO, 1st Floor, 36 Carrington Street, Sydney NSW 2000, tel: 9299 3621, fax: 9299 3808, email: <info@antosyd.org.au>.
Canada: ANTO, 2 Bloor Street West, Suite 400, Toronto, Ontario, M4W 3D2, tel: 416 967 3381, email: <travel@austria.info>.
Ireland: tel: 189 093 0118, fax: 189 093 0119, email: <holiday@austria.info>.
UK: tel: 0845 101 1818, fax: 0845 101 1819, email: <holiday@austria.info>.
US: ANTO, 120 West 45th Street, 9th Floor, New York, NY 10036; tel: 212 944 6880, fax: 212 730 4568, email: <travel@austria.info>.

TRAVELLERS WITH DISABILITIES

Salzburg Information has published a free guide called *Salzburg without Barriers*, listing all the sights, hotels and places of interest with their level of wheelchair access. It includes a map and plenty of useful information for wheelchair users. Most of the buses in the city are accessible with a wheelchair, although some of the older ones are not.

W

WEBSITES

A great deal of information about Salzburg can be obtained from the internet, and it's possible to book almost everything connected with your trip online. Some useful addresses are:

www.austria.info Austrian National Tourist Office
www.salzburginfo.at Salzburg Tourism Office
www.panoramatours.com Panorama Tours
www.salzburg-sightseeingtours.at Salzburg Sightseeing Tours
www.salzburgfestival.at Salzburg Festival
www.mozarteum.at The Mozarteum
www.polzer.at Polzer ticket office
The following attractions also have websites:
www.hangar-7.com Hangar-7
www.hausdernatur.at Haus der Natur
www.museumdermoderne.at Museum of Modern Art
www.salzburgmuseum.at Salzburg Museum (German only)
www.salzburg-zoo.at Salzburg Zoo

Y

YOUTH HOSTELS

Salzburg has a good selection of cheap youth hostels. Probably the friendliest and most popular with backpackers is YoHo, Paracelsus Strasse 9; tel: 879 649. There is also the Jugend- & Familiengästehaus (young persons' and family guesthouse) in the Josef-Preis-Allee 18, tel: 842 670. For more information on youth hostels in Salzburg, see the Austrian Youth Hostel Association website: <www.oejhw.or.at>.

Recommended Hotels

Thanks partly to the international reputation of its festivals, Salzburg has a fine selection of five-star hotels. Three- and four-star hotels tend to be a little bland – listed here are some of those that have their own charm and character. If you are on a tight budget, you will most likely need to find a *Pension* (bed and breakfast).

As Salzburg is not a huge city, even hotels slightly off the beaten track will be close enough to a bus route, and within easy reach of the city centre. Most listed below can help you organise tours and excursions around the city, while some are pick-up points on the tour routes.

You will be hard pushed to find a hotel that offers a large cooked breakfast, except the international ones. Elsewhere, breakfast is usually lighter, with bread, cereals, fruit, cold meats, cheese and yoghurt.

Prices are usually considerably higher in July and August, at Easter and for most of December. Some hotels take the opportunity to close during lulls between these peaks. Some smaller establishments, particularly Pensionen, might not accept credit cards. Our price guide is for a double room in low season with breakfast:

€€€€€	over 220 euros
€€€€	160–220 euros
€€€	100–160 euros
€€	60–100 euros
€	below 60 euros

OLD TOWN

Altstadthotel Kasererbräu €€€ *Kaigasse 33, tel: 842 445-0, <www.kasererbraeu.at>.* A charming, central hotel on Kaigasse. The rooms have a medieval feel about them and feature antique furniture, including solid wooden beds. Surprisingly, for a small central hotel, it features a luxurious wellness facility that includes a sauna and a Turkish bath. 43 rooms.

Altstadthotel Weisse Taube €€€ *Kaigasse 9, tel: 842 404, <www. weissetaube.at>.* Managed by the Wollner family, this traditional hotel is in the pedestrianised part of the Old Town, right next to Mozartplatz. It was built in 1365, on land belonging to St Peter's Abbey. Although the rooms are not particularly of any era or theme, they are basic and comfortable. Breakfast room and bar, but no restaurant. 31 rooms.

Ambiente Hotel Struber €€€ *Nonntaler Hauptstrasse 35, tel: 843 728, <www.struber.at>.* Located in the Nonntal district, behind the Old Town. Just 14 rooms, some with wooden beams, all with a rustic charm. Some have balconies with views of the fortress. Delicious home cooking.

Arthotel Blaue Gans €€€–€€€€ *Getreidegasse 41–43, tel: 842 491-0, <www.blauegans.at>.* The 'Blue Goose Art Hotel' calls itself a 'habitable work of art', and successfully fuses traditional and modern styles. The 38 rooms feature interesting works of art, crisp fabrics and warm lighting, all in a building that's nearly 700 years old.

Hotel Elefant €€€–€€€€ *Sigmund-Haffner-Gasse 4, tel: 843 397, <www.elefant.at>.* Over 700 years old, and located very centrally in the Old Town, in an alleyway off the shopping street Getreidegasse. There is a curious story that King Max of Bavaria had an elephant which stopped to look in the window of the building, since when it has been known as Elefant. The rooms are quite simple, though the focus is on comfort and subtle styling. There are two restaurants including the 17th-century Ratsherrnkeller. 32 rooms.

Hotel Goldene Ente €€€ *Goldgasse 10, tel: 845 622, <www.ente.at>.* A very central location in the Old Town, based on one of Salzburg's oldest (14th-century) inns. Rooms are decorated in the style of traditional country homes, with antiques and art on the walls. The restaurant is a favourite haunt of the locals, which means it has good traditional cooking. 15 double and 2 single rooms.

Hotel Goldener Hirsch €€€€€ *Getreidegasse 37, tel: 8084-0, <www.starwoodhotels.com>.* With only 69 rooms, this has the feeling of an elegant private home. All the rooms are unique, with their own colour schemes and themes reminiscent of a 15th-century inn, combining antique furniture and modern amenities. Guests have a choice between a gourmet international restaurant and a cosy traditional restaurant specialising in Austrian cuisine.

Schloss Mönchstein €€€€€ *Mönchsberg Park 26, tel: 848 555-0, <www.monchstein.com>*. Situated on top of the Mönchsberg and surrounded by a park, the hotel received an award for the best five-star establishment in Austria in 2004. The individualistic bedrooms and bathrooms are out of this world. Needless to say, the location offers some of the best views of the city. Only 24 rooms, so early booking is essential.

NEW TOWN

Altstadthotel Amadeus €€€ *Linzergasse 43–45, tel: 871 401, <www.hotelamadeus.at>*. Quaint and wholesome hotel in the centre of the New Town, set in a 15th-century building that has been extensively renovated in a blend of tasteful and traditional comfort. Rooms are pleasant, with rustic-style furnishings. The quietest ones are at the rear, with views of the St Sebastian Cemetery. The Amadeus Café serves drinks and bistro-style food throughout the day and evening. 26 rooms.

Altstadthotel Wolf-Dietrich €€€ *Wolf-Dietrich-Strasse 9, tel: 871 275, <www.salzburg-hotel.at>*. A homely modern hotel in an old building in a quiet quarter, yet close to the New Town attractions. Ideal for families. Very attentive service. Bio-breakfast, complimentary afternoon tea and snacks. Lovely spa and indoor pool. 40 rooms, including four Papageno and *The Magic Flute* rooms, plus one junior suite.

Austria Classic Centralhotel Gablerbräu €€€ *Linzergasse 9, tel: 889 65, <www.centralhotel.at>*. Four-storey hotel in a renovated brewery dating from the early 15th century. The traditional tavern-style restaurant, popular with Salzburgers, adds to the true Austrian experience. 51 rooms.

Austrotel Hotel Salzburg €€€€ *Mirabellplatz 8, tel: 881 688-0, <www.austrotel.at>*. Conveniently located in the centre of the New

Town, next to the Mirabell. The five-storey building was once the residence of Prince Archbishop Paris Lodron. There's an American-style lobby bar and a free coffee and juice bar (until 6pm). Breakfast served all day. Despite its history, the hotel has all the modern facilities you will need. 72 rooms.

Gasthof Auerhahn €€ *Bahnhofstrasse 15, tel: 451 052, <www.auerhahn-salzburg.at>*. A family-run establishment with simple, tasteful rooms, all 15 of which are decorated in a different way. The restaurant has won gourmet awards for several years. The shady garden offers al fresco dining in summer. Located near the railway station.

Hotel Auersperg €€€ *Auerspergstrasse 61, tel: 889 440, <www.auersperg.at>*. Family-run hotel with an old-fashioned charm and contemporary chic. Tasteful leather sofas and wooden panelling in the public rooms; bedrooms are large yet cosy. The hotel also has a roof terrace, a peaceful garden and a sauna. Breakfast only, no restaurant. 51 rooms.

Hotel Bristol €€€€€ *Makartplatz 4, tel: 873 557, <www.bristol-salzburg.at>*. Built around 1890, the Bristol is located between the Mirabell Gardens and Mozart's house. The rooms feature luxurious antique furnishings and thick-pile carpets. Expect sumptuous beds, chandeliers and rich fabrics. Fine dining in the restaurant, a cosy bar and lounge. Very close to the Paracelsus wellness centre, where special rates apply to hotel guests. 60 rooms.

Hotel Drei Kreuz €€ *Vogelweiderstrasse 9, tel: 872 790, <www.hoteldreikreuz.at>*. The name refers to the three crosses on the Kapuzinerberg. A modern, four-storey, family-run hotel featuring traditional rustic furniture and a lively bar. Breakfast room, but no restaurant. 20 rooms.

Hotel Hofwirt €€ *Schallmooser Hauptstrasse. 1, tel: 872 172-0, <www.hofwirt.net>*. A quiet hotel in a solid 100-year-old building at the top of the Linzergasse. Renovated in 2007, the rooms have a friendly, modern and stylish feel. Airy breakfast room and extravagant lobby bar. 60 rooms, one family apartment.

Hotel Mozart €€€ *Franz-Josef-Strasse 27, tel: 872 274, <www. hotel-mozart.at>.* Six-storey family-run hotel, five minutes' walk from Linzergasse and the Mirabell Gardens. Rooms are spacious – some large enough to sleep four comfortably – and cosy in a traditional, homely way. Friendly service. Breakfast only, no restaurant. 33 rooms.

Hotel Sacher €€€€€ *Schwarzstrasse 5–7, tel: 889 770, <www. sacher.com>.* Perhaps Salzburg's grandest hotel, founded in 1866 and the sister hotel to Sacher Vienna (famous for its *Sachertorte* chocolate cake). Located on the river with great views of the Old Town. The rooms range from standard to deluxe, though all are of five-star quality. The Sacher is large enough for a gym, sauna and steam bath, as well as a salon, a café and excellent restaurants serving both international cuisine and local specialities. If you look through the guest book, you will recognise many famous names. 112 rooms including suites.

Künstlerhaus € *Franz-Hinterholzer-Kai 2a, tel: (664) 341 5728, <http://web.utanet.at/kohlerw7>.* Small bed-and-breakfast in an attractive old house directly on the river with a lovely garden and the Künstlerhaus with Café Cult next door. The six rooms are basic but large and clean; not all have en-suite facilities. The garden provides some peace and quiet from the city rush.

Stadtkrug €€€ *Linzergasse 20, tel: 873 545-0, <www.stadtkrug. at>.* A popular base among performers at the Salzburg Festival, whose signed photographs adorn the walls. Rooms are sumptuously traditional with stone floors and ceiling beams. Good restaurant and roof garden with great views of the city. 35 rooms.

Stein Hotel €€€ *Giselakai 3–5, tel: 874 346-0, <www.hotelstein.at>.* Directly on the Salzach River, the newly renovated four-star hotel has been in operation since 1399. The décor is individual, some rooms with zebra themes, others with a subtle natural ambience. The grander rooms have marble bathrooms. At the top of the hotel is the famous Stein Terrace Café with commanding views over the old city and a DJ on Friday and Saturday. 55 rooms and suites.

Airport Hotel Salzburg €€€–€€€€ *Dr-M-Laireiter-Strasse 9, tel: 850 020, <www.airporthotel.at>.* A modern hotel built in traditional Alpine style, with all the facilities of a four-star hotel, including a sauna, gym and indoor pool. Located directly next to the airport (there are no flights at night) in the charming farming area of Wals. Rooms are characterless but comfortable and efficient. Restaurant, coffee-shop, bar-lounge, disco and casino. 32 rooms.

Astoria Hotel €€ *Maxglaner Hauptstrasse 7, tel: 834 277, <www. astoriasalzburg.com>.* A 15-minute walk from the city centre, the Astoria is tasteful and unpretentious. A 20th-century hotel, renovated in 2001 and reopened under new, family management. Much of the décor features modern art. Some rooms have a winter garden balcony. No restaurant but a delightful coffee-shop selling homemade cakes and other sweet treats. 30 rooms.

Doktorschössl €€ *Glaserstrasse 7 & 10, tel: 623 088, <www. doktorschloessl.com>.* A picturesque house dating from 1670, when it was home to Dr Franz Mayr, physician in ordinary to Prince Archbishop Wolf Dietrich von Raitenau and son-in-law of Santino Solari, the builder of Salzburg Cathedral. 50 spacious rooms, most of them with views of the Gaisberg or the Untersberg. Outdoor pool, pleasant garden, bar-lounge and restaurant in a vaulted hall.

Gästehaus Scheck €€ *Rennbahnstrasse 11, tel: 623 268, <www. hotel-scheck.com>.* A family-run hotel in the beautiful suburb of Aigen, east of the city, set in a stunning garden. It feels as though you are in the country, but the town centre is only a 20-minute walk away, along the banks of the Salzach River. 10 rooms with clean white walls and attractive wooden period furniture. No restaurant, breakfast only.

Haus Am Moos € *Moosstrasse 186A, tel: 824 921, <www.ammoos. at>.* A stunning private house in the picturesque semi-rural area of Moosstrasse at the foot of the Untersberg. Close to the countryside and only a 15-minute bus ride into town. It is all about the family Strassers' personal touch. High-standard rooms, all with private bathroom, and a picture-perfect garden with large pool. Breakfast room only, no restaurant.

Haus Steiner € *Moosstrasse 156C, tel: 830 031, <www.haussteiner. com>*. A beautiful Alpine-style house surrounded by the countryside, but only a 15-minute bus ride from the centre of town. Family-run, traditional Austrian hospitality. Spacious rooms with fine views; some have balconies. Cheerful breakfast room (no restaurant).

Hotel Kobenzl-Vitalhotel €€€–€€€€€ *Am Gaisberg 11, tel: 641 510, <www.kobenzl.at>*. Perched high above the city on the Gaisberg ('between Salzburg and the sky') the Kobenzl has breathtaking views. Rooms are opulent and elegant, and the Panorama restaurant serves breakfast, lunch and dinner of the highest quality. But the Kobenzl's main selling point is its health and beauty facilities: large indoor pool, saunas with steam shower, Turkish steam bath, infrared booths, and treatments ranging from Kneipp relaxation to 'colour acupuncture'. 40 rooms and suites, most with balconies.

Pension Arenberg €€€ *Blumensteinstrasse 8, tel: 640 097, <www. arenberg-salzburg.at>*. On the slopes of the Kapuzinerberg, the hotel offers a quiet retreat from the city, with the personal touch of the Leopacher family who pride themselves on traditional hosting. 13 spacious rooms, decorated in soft hues, all with balcony. Attractive garden, cheerful breakfast room (no restaurant).

Pension Elisabeth €€ *Vogelweiderstrasse 52, tel: 871 664, <www. pension-elisabeth.at>*. With some basic but very comfortable rooms and a charm of its own, this is a great place for budget travellers who still like a touch of elegance. A very bright, clean establishment. 23 rooms, some with shared facilities, and one apartment. Bicycles for rent.

Pension Sandwirt € *Lastenstrasse 6A, tel: 874 351*. Close to the railway station, this is probably the best option for travellers on a tight budget, apart from youth hostels. The 11 rooms are clean and some have en-suite facilities. The relaxing lounge and dining area are great for catching up with fellow travellers.

Recommended Restaurants

Although, on the whole, Salzburg is a relatively expensive city, eating in a restaurant remains quite inexpensive. There are, of course, the top-notch establishments that charge over the odds, but on the whole you will be able to eat delicious meals at reasonable prices.

Summer, if the weather allows, is the time for eating outdoors. Many restaurants have gardens in the summer or, at the very least, tables on the pavement. Remember, however, that we are near the Alps and that even in summer there are very few evenings when you will not need a jumper or jacket.

To help you find an eatery that suits your taste and budget some recommendations have been listed below. Cafés, which serve snacks and small meals, are also included in the list. They are classed in the cheapest category. Another option for a quick snack comes in the form of the *Würstlstand*, where the sausages are traditionally eaten standing at one of the high tables or at the counter and washed down with a beer. Many restaurants offer lunch deals. Often it is a set two-course menu at a very reasonable price. The price guide is based on a three-course evening meal per person excluding drinks and tips. Most restaurants, and some cafés, accept major credit cards.

€€€   over 40 euros
€€   15–40 euros
€   below 15 euros

OLD TOWN

RESTAURANTS

Da Pippo €€ *Alter Markt 2, tel: 843 861.* Superb Italian food with a buffet of cold starters and occasional live piano music while you eat. Located on the first floor overlooking Alter Markt; in the summer they have tables down in the square. Daily 11.30am–11pm.

Dubliner Irish Restaurant € *Kaigasse 8, tel: 909 975.* For anybody missing pub food, there is a wide choice of the usual fare from baked potatoes to fish and chips. Wash it all down with a pint of Guinness and, if the weather is good, there is outdoor seating too. Daily noon–2am.

Goldener Hirsch €€€ *Getreidegasse 37, tel: 808 40*. This famous restaurant in the very elegant hotel of the same name specialises in Austrian and international cuisine. Antique artwork and traditional decor create a relaxing atmosphere. Over the years it has won numerous accolades for its food and is the place to go for a special occasion. Daily noon–2.30pm, 6.30pm–midnight.

Humboldt Stubn' €–€€ *Gstättengasse 4–6, tel: 843 171*. A traditional restaurant and bar with an international menu and many Austrian specialities. Humboldt offers good vegetarian alternatives and excellent lunch deals. In summer there is a large, shady terrace. Daily noon–1am.

Il Sole €€ *Gstättengasse 15, tel: 843 284*. Situated next to the entrance to the Mönchsberg lift, this Italian restaurant has friendly, efficient service and good pasta and pizzas at very reasonable prices. Look out for the daily specials. Daily 11.30am–2.30pm, 5.30pm–midnight, closed Tue in spring and autumn.

Indigo € (a number of outlets throughout the city; opening times vary). These small fast-food establishments are excellent if you want a quick snack during the day while sightseeing. They offer Thai and vegetarian cuisine and some locations have indoor seating. Most restaurants are non-smoking.

Maredo €€ *Judengasse 5–7, tel: 843 894*. Fast and friendly service in this brightly lit steak and seafood restaurant. The steak and prawns can be recommended. Excellent if you are going to a show afterwards. Daily 11.30am–11.30pm.

Nagano €€ *Griesgasse 19, tel: 849 488*. Sushi restaurant situated in the centre of the Old Town. Wide choice, including meat dishes, all served in wooden boxes. Lunch deals. Daily 11.30am–3pm, 5–11pm.

Paul-Stube €€ *Herrengasse 16, tel: 843 220.* Situated in one of the narrow little alleys below the fortress, this is an old, traditional restaurant serving Austrian food. There is a garden in the summer, too. Mon–Sat 5pm–1am.

Triangel € *Wiener-Philharmoniker-Gasse 7, tel: 842 229.* A tavern-style restaurant popular with students and close to the Festival Halls. A cosy interior, and outdoor seating in summer. Mon–Sat, 11am–midnight.

Wilder Mann €€ *Getreidegasse 20, tel: 841 787.* Long wooden tables to share with the locals. The menu is Austrian and the portions are huge. The *Schnitzel* can be recommended. Mon–Sat 10am–11pm.

Zipfer Bierhaus €€ *Universitätsplatz 19, tel: 840 745.* In a 15th-century building, this traditional tavern serves Austrian food and beer in beer-hall style. The décor is quaintly old-fashioned and there is an old well to have a look at in the basement. Mon–Sat 10am–midnight; kitchen until 10pm.

Zirkelwirt €€ *Pfeifergasse 14, tel: 843 472.* An Austrian tavern with an international twist. Fabulous meals at affordable prices. One can also just go for a coffee or a beer. Daily 11am–1am.

CAFÉS

Afro Café *Bürgerspitalplatz 5, tel: 844 888.* In a very central location at the end of Griesgasse, Afro Café serves African specialities from aromatic coffees and teas to mouthwatering snacks, breakfasts, salads, soups and tapas in a colourful, fresh interior inspired by the African continent. Interesting wines from South Africa as well as Austria. Mon–Fri 10am–midnight, Sat 9am–midnight, Sun only during festival season.

Demel *Mozartplatz 2, tel: 841 403.* The famous Viennese Café Demel took over this establishment, previously known as the Café Glockenspiel. Located on the edge of one of the busiest squares in the city, the cosy café makes a great place to sit and listen to the bells chiming in the Glockenspiel opposite. But be prepared to pay over the odds for your coffee here.

Fürst *Alter Markt Brodgasse 13, tel: 843 759.* The place where the famous *Mozartkugel* was invented. A busy little café with great cakes, coffees and ice creams and a huge selection of newspapers and magazines to choose from while you relax between sightseeing expeditions. Daily May–Sept 8am–9pm, Oct–Apr 8am–8pm.

Niemetz *Herbert-von-Karajan-platz 11, tel: 843 367.* With an enviable location next to the Festival Halls, this café is a favourite with concert-goers and is full of festival memorabilia. You can sit over coffee, cake and a newspaper for as long as you like. Mon–Sat 10am–6pm.

Sigrist *Griesgasse 13, tel: 840 801.* Located on the first floor of this building, Sigrist has a terrace with a wonderful view of the river and the busy street below. Huge milk coffees and breakfast served until midday. Mon–Fri 7.30am–8pm, Sat 9am–7pm, Sun 10am–6pm.

Tomaselli *Alter Markt 9, tel: 844 488-0.* Dating from the early 18th century, Tomaselli's is the oldest café in Salzburg. It is worth a visit to see the traditionally dressed waitresses wheeling trolleys full of cakes, but it is not the cheapest or friendliest café in town. Daily 7am–9pm, during Salzburg festival until midnight.

NEW TOWN

RESTAURANTS

Bangkok €€ *Bayerhamerstrasse 33, tel: 873 688.* Excellent Thai food in a quiet little restaurant with attentive and friendly service and reasonable prices. Daily 11.30am–2.30pm, 5.30pm–11.30pm.

Die Weisse/Sudwerk €€ *Rupertgasse 2, tel: 872 246.* This restaurant incorporates a small brewery that makes its own *Weissbier* and serves excellent Austrian cuisine. Different rooms cater for different tastes and styles. Mon–Sat 10am–3am.

Shakespeare €€ *Hubert-Sattler-Gasse 3, tel: 879 106*. Easy-going, relaxed café and restaurant serving Austrian and Chinese food. Popular with students and the arty crowd. Daily 8am–2am.

Spicy-Spices € *Wolf-Dietrich-Strasse 1, tel: 870 712*. This little restaurant serves vegetarian food and also offers a take-away service. A good place for lunch, if you are in the New Town and do not want to spend too long over your meal. Mon–Sat 11am–9pm, Sun noon–9pm.

Taj Mahal €€ *Bayerhamerstrasse 13, tel: 882 010*. A popular Indian restaurant serving good curries in a relaxed atmosphere. British travellers should not expect the food to be as spicy as in some UK Indian restaurants, as Austrians prefer their curries to be on the mild side. Tue–Sun 11.30am–2pm, 5.30pm–11pm (closed for lunch Sat).

Wasserfall €€ *Linzergasse 10, tel: 873 331*. Good Italian food served in a romantic, cellar-like location. An unusual touch is the stream flowing through. Mon–Sat 5pm–midnight.

Zum fidelen Affen €€ *Priesterhausgasse 8, tel: 877 361*. Wooden tables and floors give this restaurant a warm, welcoming atmosphere. Good food, friendly service and popular with students. Mon–Sat 5pm–1am.

Zum Fleischlaberl € *Kapitelgasse 11, tel: 842 138*. This small restaurant caters mainly for locals on their lunch breaks; breakfast is also served. Home-cooked food and the best cup of tea in town. Mon–Fri 8am–5pm.

Zum Mohren €€ *Judengasse 9, tel: 840 680*. A unique restaurant in Salzburg serving three wildly different cuisines: Austrian, Italian and Indian. Centrally located, Zum Mohren offers good lunchtime deals and friendly service. Daily 11am–midnight.

CAFÉS

Bellini's *Mirabellplatz 4, tel: 871 385*. An Italian café close to the Mirabell Gardens. Serves Italian coffee and snacks. Outdoor seating. Mon–Sat 8am–1am, Sun 10am–1am.

Café Bazar *Schwarzstrasse 3, tel: 874 278*. Slightly expensive, but with a lovely terrace overlooking the river. The art deco interior has been elegantly renovated. Sit and watch the world go by as all the famous literary figures in Salzburg did. Mon–Sat 7.30am–11pm, Sun 9am–6pm.

Café Classic *Makartplatz 8, tel: 882 700*. Located in Mozart's townhouse, this café is very much along the lines of a Viennese coffee house. Wonderful cakes and frothy coffee. Daily 7.30am–7.30pm.

Café Confiserie Sacher *Schwarzstrasse 5–7, tel: 889 770*. A sister of the famous Café Sacher in Vienna and 'inventor' of the chocolate cake of the same name. Treat yourself to a wonderful moist slice of this cake, or order a meal. In summer, there is a terrace on the river. Daily 7.30am–midnight.

Daimler's Bar Lounge *Giselakai 17, tel: 873 967*. A romantic Italian lounge, part of a lively, popular bar and overlooking the river. The food is traditional Italian pizzas and baguettes. Sun–Wed 9pm–4am, Thur–Sat 9pm–5am.

Fingerlos *Franz-Josef-Strasse 9, tel: 874 213*. Best ever coffee and cakes, all made on the premises. This is a popular place for breakfast too, if not the cheapest. The décor is modern and bright and in summer there are tables on the pavement. Tue–Sun 7.30am–7.30pm.

Steinterrasse *Giselakai 3–5, tel: 874 346-0*. Part of a trendy hotel, this is one of the in places of Salzburg and a great place for people-watching. The terrace affords a panoramic view of the city and in the evenings you can get what are considered to be the best cocktails in town. Daily 9am–midnight.

RESTAURANTS

AugustinerBräu € *Augustinergasse 4, tel: 431 246.* Genuine beer-hall atmosphere in a brewery founded by Augustinian monks. Wonderful beer, beautiful garden and plenty of snacks to choose from. You can even bring your own picnic. Mon–Fri 3–11pm, Sat–Sun and holidays 2.30–11pm.

Bärenwirt €€ *Müllner Hauptstrasse 8, tel: 430 386-0.* A traditional restaurant serving Austrian cuisine, vegetarian and wholegrain food. There has been a restaurant on this site for over 350 years. Thur–Tue 11am–2pm, 6–11pm.

Esszimmer €€€ *Müllner Hauptstrasse 33, tel: 870 899.* Fine dining in a lovely location. This Michelin-rated restaurant has an excellent reputation, and its relaxed atmosphere makes it a popular place. Vegetarians are well catered for and there is a quiet garden in summer. Tue–Sat noon–2pm, 6.30pm–midnight (food served until 10pm), Aug and Dec open Mon.

Hotel Friesacher €€ *Brunngasse 1, Anif, tel: (6246) 8977.* Friesacher has an excellent reputation as one of the best traditional restaurants serving Austrian food, wine and beer. Although slightly out of the city in Anif, the hotel restaurant is worth making the journey here, particularly if you are visiting Hellbrunn.

Ikarus €€€ *Hangar-7, Wilhelm-Spazier-Strasse 7a, tel: 219 777.* This is a restaurant with a difference. Enjoy a first-class meal with a view of the Red Bull collection of vintage aircraft in Hangar-7. Top guest chefs from around the world spend a month at a time cooking up delights. Reservations necessary. Daily noon–2pm, 6.30pm–10pm.

Krimpelstätter €€ *Müllner Hauptstrasse 31, 432 274.* A traditional tavern with a beer garden serving good Austrian food. Very popular with the festival crowd. Tue–Sat 11am–midnight, Sun 11am–3pm.

Lemon Chilli €€ *Nonntaler Hauptstrasse 24, tel: 842 558.* A Tex-Mex restaurant whose kitchen turns out good food and bar creates excellent cocktails – all amid a lively atmosphere. Popular with students. Garden in the summer. Reservations recommended. Daily 5pm–1am.

Lin's Garden €€ *Leopoldskronstrasse 1, tel: 846 356.* Very friendly Chinese restaurant a few minutes' walk from the Old Town. It has a charming walled garden and excellent lunch offers. Tue–Sat 11.30am–2.30pm, 5.30pm–midnight.

Poseidon €€ *Neutorstrasse 34, tel: 842 918.* Probably Salzburg's best Greek restaurant. It is very popular and reservations are recommended. All your favourite Greek dishes served in warm and welcoming surroundings. There is a lovely garden in the summer. Daily 11.30am–3pm, 5.30pm–1am.

Riedenburg €€€ *Neutorstrasse 31, tel: 843 923.* This is considered by some to be the best restaurant in Salzburg. It has a Michelin star and serves wonderful food, beautifully presented. Try the three-course lunch menu for less than €20. The wine list is also exquisite. Reservations recommended. Tue–Sat noon–2pm, 6pm–midnight.

Wastlwirt €€ *Rochusgasse 15, Maxlglam, tel: 820 100.* Located in a quiet corner, not far from the city centre, this traditional tavern is wonderfully cosy with lots of wood and a leafy, shady garden. Mon–Fri 10am–midnight.

CAFÉS

Café am Kai *Müllner Hauptstrasse 4, tel: 420 565.* With a terrace overlooking the river, this lovely pink café is a good place to take a break when walking along the river. Wed–Mon 9am–8pm.

Carpe Diem Lounge *Hangar-7, Wilhelm-Spazier-Strasse 7a, tel: 219 70.* An elegantly furnished café housed under the glass dome of Hangar-7. Enjoy your coffee while watching the goings-on in the museum through the glass wall. Daily 9am–7pm.

INDEX

Accommodation 105, 128–34
Aldstadt 34–49
Alter Markt 42–3
Augustinerbräu 49

Berchtesgaden (Germany) 67–8
Salt Mines 68

Capuchin Monastery 57–8
Cathedral 37–8
Cathedral Museum 38
Chapel of St Gabriel 51
Chiemseehof 33
Collegiate Church 44

Domplatz 37

Eagle's Nest 68
Easter Festival 84
Eisriesenwelt Caves 72–3

Felix Gate 57
Felsenreitschule 45
festivals 84–6, 93
Festival Halls (Festspielhäuser) 44–5
Festung Hohensalzburg 28–31
Föhn, The 63
Fortress Museum 30
Franciscan Church 45–6
Fuschlsee 77–8

Getreidegasse 43
Glossglockner High Alpine Road 73–5
Grödig 65

Grosses Festspielhaus (Large Festival Hall) 45
Grossgmain Open-air Museum 65
Gstättengasse 46

Hallein 70–1
Celtic Village 70
Dürrnberg Salt Mines 70
Silent Night Museum 71
Hangar-7 59–60
Haus der Natur (Natural History Museum) 47
Hellbrunn Palace 60–3
Folklore Museum 62
Salzburg Zoo 62
Stone Theatre 62
Hohensalzburg Fortress see Festung Hohensalzburg
Hohenwerfen Castle 71–2
House for Mozart 45

Judengasse 42

Kaigasse 33
Kajetanerplatz 33
Kapitelplatz 36
Kapuzinerberg 57
Karneval 85
Kehlsteinhaus see Eagle's Nest
Klessheim Palace 63
Königssee (Germany) 68–9
Krimml Waterfalls 76–7

Lake District 77–81
Landestheater 53
Large Festival Hall 45
Leopoldskron Palace 58–9
Linzergasse 50

Makartplatz 51–2
Marionette Museum 31
Marionettentheater 53
Mirabell Palace 54–6
Mönchsberg 27–33
Mondsee 81
Mozart, Wolfgang Amadeus 20, 40–1, 43–4, 52–3, 78, 83
Mozarteum 52
Mozart Memorial Room (St Gilgen) 79
Mozartplatz 41
Mozart's Birthplace 43–4
Mozart's Residence 51–3
Mozart Statue 13, 41, 46
Mülln 49
Museum der Moderne (Museum of Modern Art) 48

Neptune's Fountain 36
Neue Residenz 40
New Town 50–8
nightlife 86–7
Nonnberg Convent 31–2
Nonntaler Hauptstrasse 33

Obersalzberg 67
Old Town see Altstadt

Pferdeschwemme
(Horse Pond and
Fountain) 44

Rainer-Regiments-
Museum 30
Reinhardt, Max 22
Residenz 39
Residenzplatz 39
Rottmayr, Johann
Michael 38
Rupertinum 45

St Erhard im Nonntal 33
St Gilgen 78–9
St John's Chapel 32
St Kajetan 33

St Mark's Church 46–7
St Peter's Abbey 34–5
St Peter's Stiftskeller 35
St Sebastian's
Church 50–1
St Wolfgang 79–80
Salzburg Card 9
Salzburger
Barockmuseum 54
Salzburg Festival 84, 124
Salzburg Museum 40
Salzburg Zoo 62
Salzkammergut 77–81
shopping 87–8
Sound of Music, The
32, 54, 56, 59, 62,
78, 81, 87

Spielzeugmuseum (Toy
Museum) 48
sports 89–92
Stations of the
Cross 57
Stiegl's Brauwelt 60

Universitätsplatz 44
Untersberg 64–6
Ursulinenplatz 46

Werfen 71–2
Whitsun
Festival 84
Wolfgangsee 78–81

Zweig, Stefan 58

Berlitz pocket guide

Salzburg

Second Edition 2008
Reprinted 2010

Written by Leigh-Anne Coetzee,
Nicola Gander and Eleanor Fitzgerald
Updated by Trudie Trox
Principal photographer: Britta Jaschinski
Edited by Alex Knights and Jeffery Pike
Series Editor: Tony Halliday

Photography credits
All photography by Britta Jaschinski except
Leigh-Anne Coetzee 26; Annabel Elston and
John Spaull 32, 46, 64, 72; Ulrich Grill/redbull-
photofiles.com 59; Tony Halliday 15, 28, 29, 34;
Bildagentur Huber 67, 69; Imagno/Getty Images
10, 17, 23; Salzburg Festival: Oskar Anrather 84,
Clärchen and Matthias Baus 82, Fritz Haseke 24,
53; Salzburg Tourist Office 1, 8, 37, 41, 61, 92, 103;
Mozart Museum, Salzburg/Topfoto 21

Cover picture: Imagestate

Every effort has been made to provide
accurate information in this publication,
but changes are inevitable. The publisher
cannot be responsible for any resulting
loss, inconvenience or injury.

Contact us

At Berlitz we strive to keep our guides as
accurate and up to date as possible, but if you
find anything that has changed, or if you have
any suggestions on ways to improve this guide,
then we would be delighted to hear from you.

Berlitz Publishing, PO Box 7910,
London SE1 1WE, England.
fax: (44) 20 7403 0290
email: berlitz@apaguide.co.uk
www.berlitzpublishing.com